The Shakespeare Handbooks

THE SHAKESPEARE HANDBOOKS

Series Editor: John Russell Brown

PUBLISHED

FORTHCOMING

The Shakespeare Handbooks

The Merchant of Venice

Christopher McCullough

palgrave
macmillan

First published 2005 by
PALGRAVE MACMILLAN
Houndmills, Basingstoke, Hampshire RG21 6XS and
175 Fifth Avenue, New York, N.Y. 10010
Companies and representatives throughout the world

PALGRAVE MACMILLAN is the global academic imprint of the Palgrave Macmillan division of St. Martin's Press, LLC and of Palgrave Macmillan Ltd. Macmillan® is a registered trademark in the United States, United Kingdom and other countries. Palgrave is a registered trademark in the European Union and other countries.

ISBN-13: 978–1–4039–3959–3   hardback
ISBN 10: 1–4039–3959–4   hardback
ISBN-13: 978–1–4039–3960–9   paperback
ISBN 10: 1–4039–3960–8   paperback

This book is printed on paper suitable for recycling and made from fully managed and sustained forest sources.

A catalogue record for this book is available from the British Library.

Library of Congress Cataloging-in-Publication Data

McCullough, Christopher, M.A.
      The merchant of Venice / Christopher McCullough.
          p. cm.—(Shakespeare handbooks)
      Includes bibliographical references and index.
      ISBN-13: 978-1-4039-3959-3 (alk. paper)
      ISBN-10: 1-4039-3959-4 (alk. paper)
      ISBN-13: 978-1-4039-3960-9 (pbk.: alk. paper)
      ISBN-10: 1-4039-3960-8 (pbk.: alk. paper)
          1. Shakespeare, William, 1564–1616. Merchant of Venice.
      2. Venice (Italy)—In literature. 3. Shylock (Fictitious character)
      4. Jews in literature. 5. Comedy. I. Title. II. Shakespeare handbooks
      (Palgrave)
      PR2825.M225 2005
      822.3'3—dc22
                                                              2005048761

10   9   8   7   6   5   4   3   2   1
14   13   12   11   10   09   08   07   06   05

Printed and bound in China

For Becca and Anna

Contents

A Note on the Text

Unless otherwise stated, all quotations and references to *The Merchant of Venice* are from the edition by John Russell Brown (London: Methuen, 1967). All other quotations from Shakespeare's plays are from the edition by Stanley Wells and Gary Taylor (Oxford: Oxford University Press, 1986).

General Editor's Preface

The Shakespeare Handbooks provide an innovative way of studying the theatrical life of the plays. The commentaries, which are their core feature, enable a reader to envisage the words of a text unfurling in performance, involving actions and meanings not readily perceived except in rehearsal or performance. The aim is to present the plays in the environment for which they were written and to offer an experience as close as possible to an audience's progressive experience of a production.

While each book has the same range of contents, their authors have been encouraged to shape them according to their own critical and scholarly understanding and their first-hand experience of theatre practice. The various chapters are designed to complement the commentaries: the cultural context of each play is presented together with quotations from original sources; the authority of its text or texts is considered with what is known of the earliest performances; key performances and productions of its subsequent stage history are both described and compared. The aim in all this has been to help readers to develop their own informed and imaginative view of a play in ways that supplement the provision of standard editions and are more user-friendly than detailed stage histories or collections of criticism from diverse sources.

Further volumes are in preparation so that, within a few years, the Shakespeare Handbooks will be available for all the plays that are frequently studied and performed.

John Russell Brown

Preface: Formulating Models for Performance

This volume, with theatrical practice at its metaphorical centre, attempts to address a debate about the ways in which we begin to understand how culture is made, and indeed, recognizes the notion that there is never an end to the process of making and remaking. We need to be able to understand how *The Merchant of Venice* was of its age, and how, without necessarily 'being for all ages' in any essentialist sense, it is re-made time and time again. As I write this preface, there are many *Merchants* being rehearsed and produced around the world, either on stages, or through the vehicles of new media. Culture does not stand still, but may be understood as necessarily engaged in a continuing process of new meaning.

The ordering of chapters in this volume of the series is slightly out of kilter with the general trend. The aim in placing the Commentary (Chapter 6) at the end of the volume has one purpose in that it is the main focus of the book. All the other chapters function as preparatory detail embedding the play in the various cultural practices that have created the play's meaning through the last four centuries. This Commentary is presented, however, so that it can be consulted directly when seeking to understand the theatrical implications of any passage in the play text.

C.M.

Acknowledgements

As always, many people contribute to any volume, even if it is only a passing remark in the corridor. However, first and foremost, I thank my friend and colleague Peter Thomson for his time and patience; his high standards are a continual reminder to me of how much I still have to learn. Thank you also to Tony Sher for his time, wit and good companionship. My thanks are also due to the University of Exeter in allowing me a period of study leave. Any series such as this that breaks new ground in introducing the reader to the various ways and means by which we read a play theatrically, usually has a driving imagination behind it. This series is no exception, and I would finally like to thank John Russell Brown, whose energy and sharp eye have kept me to the mark of the series' purpose.

Acknowledgments

1 Textual History and Dates

There is little doubt that we need, when we think about the working practices of early modern theatre, to dispense with many of our modern (nineteenth century onwards) assumptions regarding dramatic and theatrical practice.

A number of interesting questions are raised regarding the making of sixteenth- and early seventeenth-century theatre when we consider the spelling of the noun 'playwright'. Is playwriting an art or a craft? Is acting an art or a craft? And, if there is art in theatre, where does its provenance lie? This chapter will offer an account of the historical development of the play text we know as *The Merchant of Venice*, but to do so, we must also consider how we understand plays and theatre in the cultural context of Shakespeare's professional life.

Etymologically, the word 'playwright' is related to nouns that are normally associated, unambiguously, with various crafts: 'wheelwright' and 'shipwright' being the most obvious examples. Recently, Peter Thomson has, in pointing out the spelling of 'playwright' in his essay on 'Conventions of Playwriting', contextualized the production of play texts in the material and commercial business of working to commission and deadline, producing work to meet the needs of a company's season, and taking account of who was working in a company at a particular time (Thomson, 2003, pp. 46–54). A play in Shakespeare's working life was a thing 'wrought' to meet the current needs of a working professional company of players. All of the evidence would seem to point to a society where there was little distinction between art and craft, and, in the case of Shakespeare's theatre, the term 'literary' does not carry much significance, particularly in the modern sense of the word. Raymond Williams argues that 'In its modern form, the concept of "literature" did not emerge earlier than the eighteenth century and was not fully developed until the nineteenth century' (R. Williams, 1977, pp. 46–7). This is not to say that literary works did not exist in the Renaissance, but that they were not identified in a way that is generally accepted in the modern era.

The theatres and companies that developed, and in many cases thrived, after 1576, when the first successful purpose-built playhouse opened in London, evolved what we may assume were fairly standard practices in the production of their plays. All theatre, extending as it does beyond the bounds of language, writing and individual expression into the properties of visual signs and collective performance between actors, and most importantly, between actors and spectators, sits uneasily within the generally understood methods by which literature is produced. With regard to Elizabethan stage practices, I propose a distinction between a script and a text.

A script, as I wish to define it in this context, was the original encoding of the play's narrative and kept to as few copies as possible for fear of pirating by ad hoc travelling players (although Queen Elizabeth had enacted legislation in the 1570s against travelling players, they still operated in the provinces, particularly in times of plague in London, as we may see if we look at the frontispiece of the 1603 First Quarto of *Hamlet*). The professional practice most often entailed a writer and a company meeting to decide on the company's new repertoire. The process that followed was driven by the needs of the playing company, rather than any privileged notion of a writer's individual creative vision. This is not to say that individual creative vision was lacking. Rather, the need is to contextualize the working practices of the period, and to place them firmly in the material business of running a theatre and producing theatrical events to please the theatre-going public. Furthermore, any new play had to fit within the range of skills present in the company of players. For example, if there was a known and popular specialist clown, then there must be a role to amuse him and the audience. Nor should we forget that the length of a play was determined by the playing conditions of the public playhouse: the 'two hours traffic' of the stage. Once an agreement between company and writer was reached, the writer produced a handwritten copy now referred to as the 'author's foul papers', which may or may not have contained a number of corrections necessitating clean copies to be produced by a scribe (the 'fair copy'). We may assume that there were only two of what I choose to term 'script' copies: one became the promptbook holder's copy, which could often be the source for the printed quarto and/or folio copies of the play, and the other copy was divided into players' parts, with appropriate cue lines added. Once the authority of the Master of the Revels was confirmed, a *third* copy may have been prepared for him to read prior to the licensing of performance. The idea of printing the 'script', for purposes of protection, revision, distribution and, possibly, reading generally, did not take place until after the play's successful run on the stage of the playhouse (that is, its commercial life) was over. We may then argue that the script was transformed from an intrinsic element in the stage practices of the company into a proto-literary text.

There are no consistent patterns to the history of Shakespeare's plays after the companies' initial performances. Some plays, such as *Hamlet*, have clear textual histories: the First Quarto (also known as the Bad Quarto) of 1603, the Second Quarto of 1604 and the First Folio of 1623. It is generally accepted that the two latter printings are the most reliable. Plays such as *Romeo and Juliet* even have five quarto versions of varying degrees of reliability. *King Lear* appears in a quarto form of 1608 that is distinctly different from the later 1623 folio printing. Until recently, many editors conflated the two on the assumption that the two versions both, imperfectly, represent a single play, but recent scholarship claims them to be two separate plays, the latter, the Folio, being a revision by Shakespeare of the 1608 Quarto (Wells and Taylor, 1986).

Despite the mounting evidence that the plays were intrinsically part of the material practice of contemporary stagecraft, the cultural process of the last 400 years has tended to ignore this evidence and to appropriate the plays into literature as written poetry. In the twentieth century the most eminent prosecutor of the literary case was the poet T. S. Eliot. He has been followed by a seemingly endless stream of academics, usually in university departments of English, who, if they give any credence at all to the performance of Shakespeare's plays, do so only to help the less able student on the road to a deeper understanding through close critical reading. What such critics seemingly fail to recognize is that the complex relationship between Elizabethan stage practice and emergent literary forms indicates that culture in the late sixteenth and early seventeenth centuries stood at the threshold of the modern world where practices, political, commercial, ideological and aesthetic, were in an embryonic form that was to evolve through western European industrialization. As the plays of Shakespeare were transmuted from the 'base metal' of pre-literary performance script into the 'gold' of the post-theatrical documentation of the theatrical artefact as literary text, we may perceive a tension between script and text, at least at the level of critical reception.

There seems little to be gained by espousing an oppositional stance in which performance is set against literature. Nor is there much to be gained by exacerbating the tension – that unfortunately does exist – by adopting one position in order to deny the efficacy of the other. I assume no mystical primacy of speech and action over writing, nor of the printed word over speech and action. The late sixteenth century did herald a revolution in the development of the printed word into what we may now recognize as literature (in Shakespeare's case, poetry), but this was the production of evolving ideology at the time. A recognizably 'modern' world was in the making as may be observed in the development of a mercantile society, which formed the foundation for the later development of capitalism. Postwar directors of *The Merchant of Venice* have often been tempted into depicting the sixteenth-century mercantile ideology of the play's Venice as a site of late nineteenth-century high capitalism, which is, in the end, the imposition of later ideological structures on early modern England. This is a subject that will be discussed in greater detail in the next chapter.

We must accept that text and production have evolved as separate, but not necessarily competing, formations. Terry Eagleton points out that 'text and production are distinct formations – different natural modes of production, between which no homologous or "reproductive" relationship can hold' (Eagleton, 1978). Put simply, we gain nothing by insisting on the extant 'literary' text functioning as the aesthetic yardstick by which to judge the performance, nor should we hope to claim an ontological priority of live performance over close reading.

On 22 July 1598 the following entry was made in the Stationers' Register:

> Entered for his copy under the hands of both the wardens, a book of the Merchant of Venice or other wise called the Jew of Venice. Provided that it be not printed by the said James Roberts; or any other whatsoever without licence first had from the Right honourable the Lord Chamberlain. vjd   (Register C, fol. 39 verso; Greg, 1939)

However, the earliest received text of *The Merchant of Venice* is a quarto printing dated 1600. Why was there a delay of two years in the printing and publishing of *The Merchant of Venice* before, on 28 October 1600, Thomas Haies entered a 'book' called the book of *The Merchant of Venyce*? We may never know for certain what facts lie behind this delay, but, if we look at the situation from the other way around and focus not on the delay itself, but on the reason for an early submission, we may surmise that the early entry of 1598 was to prevent any pirating of the Lord Chamberlain's Men's play book. John Russell Brown, in the introduction to his edition of the play, suggests that, as James Roberts (in whose name the play had been entered in 1598) was more a printer than a publisher, he took more plays than he was able to print in order to secure the rights, but may eventually have transferred the rights to other publishers such as Thomas Haies (Brown, 1967, p. xii). Either way, it would seem that there were very practical material reasons for the initial submission and subsequent delay in the publishing.

The mention of a 'book' of *The Merchant of Venyce* is intriguing. Are we to suppose that this 'book' was the company's promptbook? If so, the first printing and publishing of the play may have been derived from what is a form of metatext: that is the promptbook with all of its stage directions (the metatext) intact. The notion of stage directions as a form of metatext that indicates a woven (or wrought) textuality beyond words on the page is exemplified in John Russell Brown's 1600 Quarto-based edition. For example:

[ACT II]

[SCENE I. – *Belmont.*]

[Flourish Cornets.] Enter [the Prince of] MOROCCO *(a tawny Moor all
in white), and three or four followers accordingly, with* PORTIA,
NERISSA, *and their train.*

This example offers a sense of the peopling of the stage. If Portia and
Nerissa have three or four followers in their train as well as the three
or four indicated for the Prince of Morocco, the stage has to accommodate eleven players, who are required to enter with a flourish. We
may accept that the stage of the Globe theatre was of similar dimensions to that of the Fortune (43 feet wide and approximately 27 feet
deep), so there isn't a huge problem of crowd choreography.
However, the relatively recent discoveries on the site of the Rose
theatre, as so succinctly presented by Carol Rutter, may give pause
for thought when we learn that the stage, in both its earlier and later
architecture, was considerably smaller than that of the Globe (Rutter,
1999, pp. ix–xv). This would have meant that the stage in that theatre
would have become crowded by the simultaneous presence of eleven
players. As many scholars point out, costume was the significant
visual element on the London stage of the time, and those costumes
(such as farthingales worn by men playing women) took up a considerable amount of space. We may believe the Globe stage to have
been larger than that of the Rose, but the problem is still one to be
considered.

Again, we may consider the metatextual function of the stage
direction, in the same edition, as follows:

[ACT II]

[SCENE V. – *Venice. Before Shylock's House.*]

*Enter [*SHYLOCK *the]* Jew *and [*LAUNCELOT*]* his man that was the
clown.

John Russell Brown notes that, 'Either (1) there should be a comma
after *was*, and *the clown* be a further description of the character, or (2)

Launcelot has ceased to be merely a rustic "clown" and now appears in the motley "guarded" coat of a fool of Bassanio's household.'

The prompt book 'script' may, then, have furnished the material for the first 'text'. Alternatively, John Russell Brown proposes in his introduction to his edition that the 1600 Quarto was more likely to have been printed from either the author's foul papers or a fair copy of those papers. If the play was still in the regular repertory when Roberts received a copy, it may be, as he argues, that the copy would have to be one that the company could spare, which is unlikely to have been a promptbook as that would be needed for performance. Furthermore, a number of the stage directions do not specify the number of players making an entrance. This factor, it is argued, makes it more likely that the copy from which the First Quarto is derived was the author's foul papers, or a fair copy of those, as the prompt copy would be more likely to contain the precise numbers to be arranged on stage. Whatever the facts of the matter may be, for those of us wishing to work as closely as we can to the 'script' that led performance, the possibility of the 1600 Quarto being derived from either a promptbook or the author's papers offers a tantalizing glimpse into the theatrical event itself.

There is no evidence to show that *The Merchant of Venice* was printed again in quarto format until 1619. Because many of the typographical peculiarities are the same as those of the 1600 Quarto, it is generally assumed that this quarto is simply a reprint of the original. The third printing of *The Merchant of Venice* was in the First Folio of 1623, which in its turn produced folio printings in 1663 and 1685, with a further quarto in 1637. As our purpose is to focus on the practical business of the stage practices associated with this play, we may do no more than register these re-printings, as they offer little by way of significant change from the 1600 Quarto, the text that takes us so tantalizingly close to the play in its original performance context.

The production of a play in print cannot be divorced, practically or, in broader terms, culturally, from its production as a theatrical event. The reason for this book's existence rests on the premise that you, the reader, and I the author, are entering on a project from which we hope to gain a deeper understanding of a play, generally known as *The Merchant of Venice*, but which may also have been known as *The Jew of Venice*, probably written by William Shakespeare (possibly Shagspere, as English spelling of the time was as slippery as is the identity of the original text). Already there are two of us engaged in the making of this play, but, in order to reach a fuller understanding, we must call in the resources, the evidence, of many people past and present. The text employed by this exploration will be the edition produced by John Russell Brown (still in print) and based on the 1600 First Quarto. Editing a work implies that the effort is towards an authoritative text that most nearly represents the author's original work. However, since we have already admitted to the uncertainty of the play's provenance from first idea, through the various forms of 'papers' and 'scripts', through actors' extemporizations, to printers' technologies and the whims of publishers, we are implicitly accepting the notion that the 'text' – in whatever form we experience it – is the result of a rich range of creative collaborations (we may, of course, add to the list: carpenters, painters, stage managers, as collaborators in the enterprise).

Finally, we return to the original point of the spelling of 'playwright' and the intricate weaving of the play in our contemporary sensing of it. By way of a postscript, it is worth noting that in recent history there have been two adaptations of *The Merchant of Venice*: *Variations on The Merchant* by Charles Marowitz (1978), and an adaptation also entitled *The Merchant* (1976) by Arnold Wesker. That these two modern playwrights are Jewish is germane to further explorations of Shakespeare's play, and the matter of Shylock is one that we will not seek to avoid in the ensuing chapters.

2 Intellectual and Cultural Context

A fairly standard brief description of the play's provenance might run thus: written about 1596–7, published in quarto form in 1600 with the title page: 'The most excellent History of the Merchant of Venice. With the extreme cruelty of Shylock the Jew towards the said Merchant, in cutting a just pound of his flesh: and the obtaining of Portia by the choice of three chests. As it has been diverse times acted by the Lord Chamberlain his servants. Written by William Shakespeare.' While there is nothing out of order in this description, it achieves little by way of telling us about the cultural context of this play's making, the play's cultural sources, the kind of historical distance between us and the play, or, indeed, why we still perform a play that is over 400 years old. The next stage in our exploration of *The Merchant of Venice* will afford us the opportunity to observe the intellectual and cultural context of the play's making, and the subsequent historical distance that has engendered the continuous re-making of the play.

The source of the bond theme in the play was *Il Pecarone* (The Simpleton), attributed to Ser Giovanni of Florence, and the idea of the caskets was derived from Richard Robinson's version of the *Gesta Romanorum*. The play also contains some parallels to Christopher Marlowe's *Jew of Malta*.

Il Pecarone is one of some fifty Italian stories written in the later years of the fourteenth century and must have served as the main source of the plot for Shakespeare's play. It is of interest to note that no sixteenth-century English translation is known, so unless there is a lost version, Shakespeare must have read the story in the original

Italian. Apart from shedding possible light on Shakespeare's linguistic skills, this alerts us to the ways in which the development of the distinct English nation state under Elizabeth I was matched by the increase in trade, both cultural and commercial, between European nations; the latter point surely having bearing on themes in *The Merchant of Venice*. In the story of *Il Pecarone*, a highborn beautiful widow of Belmonte (the Portia figure) challenges suitors to seduce her. If they fail to please her, they suffer forfeiture of their goods. By drugging them as they retire to bed, she ensures that they sleep soundly and fail to please her sexually. By this means, she grows rich. Giannetto (Bassanio) has twice encountered this lady and succumbed both to her charms and to her drugs, and twice lost the fortune given to him by his Godfather Ansaldo (Antonio). Giannetto is resolved to try once more, but to enable him to accomplish this, Ansaldo has to raise the money by borrowing from a Jew. The rest of the story, the bond of the pound of flesh, Giannetto winning the lady and the lady rescuing Ansaldo from the knife by disguising herself as a lawyer, is more or less the story we know from Shakespeare. One significant difference is that the story of the caskets is missing from *Il Pecarone*. This element of the plot Shakespeare gleaned from an anonymous anthology entitled the *Gesta Romanorum*. In this story a maid who wishes to marry the son of the Emperor of Rome must choose from three vessels, of gold, silver and lead, each marked with inscriptions markedly similar to the inscriptions on Portia's caskets. The maid chooses lead and wins the hand of the Emperor's son.

These then are the main literary sources from which Shakespeare worked in creating *The Merchant of* Venice. However, there are many different ways by which we may approach the historical and cultural provenance of a play. When we are dealing with the matter of Shakespeare and the sixteenth- and early seventeenth-century theatre, we must also be aware of how history has created a Shakespeare and an Elizabethan world that bears very slight relationship to the world that emerges from a close historiographical analysis. Equally, we observe – and this will be examined further in Chapter 3 – how the meaning attributed to the play has changed through history. Given the centrality of the cultural place afforded to Shakespeare and his works, we do need to understand that

Shakespeare now is not just the man who lived in the late sixteenth century. We now accept that there is Shakespeare the cultural icon, as well as Shakespeare the playwright, poet and actor. The sonnet 'Shakespeare' by Matthew Arnold (first published in 1849) is a useful example in demonstrating how Shakespeare the man has been transformed into a cultural icon with spiritual overtones.

Shakespeare
Others abide our question. Thou art free.
We ask and ask: Thou smilest and art still,
Out-topping knowledge. For the loftiest hill
That to the stars uncrowns his majesty,
Planting his steadfast footsteps in the sea,
Making the Heaven of Heavens his dwelling-place,
Spares but the cloudy border of his base
To the foil'd searching of mortality:
And thou, who didst the stars and sunbeams know,
Self-school'd, self-scann'd, self-honour'd, self-secure,
Didst walk on Earth unguess'd at. Better so!
All the pains the immortal spirit must endure,
   All weakness that impairs, all griefs that bow,
   Find their sole voice in that victorious brow.

This transformation is sometimes referred to as Bardolatry, which means the linking of the man of Elizabethan and Jacobean theatre with the images of the Bard (of Avon) and idolatry. Arnold's sonnet suggests this and even risks, in the lines 'Self-school'd, self-scann'd, self-honour'd, self-secure, / Didst walk on Earth unguess'd at', the association of Shakespeare with an image suggestive of Christ. The man of history becomes transcendent of that history and acquires metaphysical overtones.

We may, in attempting to understand Arnold's meaning, gain some insight when we understand that Arnold (particularly some twenty or so years later when he wrote his major piece of social criticism, *Culture and Anarchy*, and works on the future of religious faith in an increasingly sceptical age) was seeking spiritual values in the intrinsic aesthetic values of secular art. This perceived transformation of Shakespeare into a cultural icon central to English cultural values owes much to the development and purpose of art in nine-teenth-century England, where art, and in particular poetry, became the repository of spiritual values, as institutionalized religion appeared to wane.

Shakespeare himself, by the processes of history, becomes a 'text' to be read critically, with the understanding that 'text' in this sense is both similar and dissimilar to the notion of the literary text argued in the last chapter. The similarity rests upon the idea of a text as a thing woven and in that sense 'Shakespeare', the cultural icon, while being the man, is also a woven cultural text that fulfils many of the differ-ent aims and ambitions of the ages that have encountered and created him. Ben Jonson, in describing Shakespeare as 'not for an age, but for all time', was not necessarily referring to an essentialist notion of historical transcendence (how could he foretell the future?). He also wrote, in the same essay, 'For a poet's made, as well as born.' It is essential to the purpose of this chapter that we seek an understand-ing of the 'intellectual and cultural context' of Shakespeare's making, as well as the making and re-making of *The Merchant of Venice*. Furthermore, as we are dealing with the span of historical distance between our own society and that of the later sixteenth and early seventeenth centuries, we must, of necessity, encounter the different 'times' of their making.

When we read a text on the page, we have already been party to an inevitable change in textual meaning and replication. The words on the page may remain unaltered, but the text has entered our percep-tion and, in discourse, will undergo as much iteration as there are readers and discourses. Of course, when the initial experience is a performance, the process is further complicated (refined?) by each spectator receiving something different from the events on stage, which are, anyway, going to be changing in subtle ways in each performance, for each age and all time.

A play by Shakespeare, no matter which extant scholarly textual edition we encounter, has embedded in it the enscriptions of theatri-cal processes then and now (whenever we mean by 'then'). Edward Said in *Culture and Imperialism* appropriates T. S. Eliot's notion of the aesthetic (in Eliot's case) value in recognizing 'pastness'. Said explains Eliot's concern with 'the need to fully comprehend the pastness of the past in order to understand that there is no way the past can be quarantined from the present'. Said continues, 'Eliot's synthesis of the past, present and future, however, is idealistic . . . and its conception of time leaves out the combativeness with which individuals decide on what is tradition and what is not, what is relevant and what not' (Said, 1994, pp. 2–3).

In addition to Edward Said, we may also consider the possibilities raised in Robert Weimann's phrase 'past significance and present meaning', in the Introduction to his recent book *Author's Pen and Actor's Voice*. In this context, Weimann argues for what we may term the recognition, even the sensuality, of historical distance and difference, rejecting potentially facile analogies between then and now.

> Analogies between then and now carry perils; the facile establishment of similitude invites at best self-projection, at worst self-congratulation. It is an entirely different matter, however, to grapple with what elsewhere I have called the ineluctable conjuncture of 'past significance and present meaning'. The idea is not simply to read and revitalize Shakespeare through our own haunting concerns or to use our sense of contemporaneity as a probe into previously underestimated or obliterated uses of his plays; rather, there is a simultaneous and equally urgent need to disclose the liabilities and uncertainties in our own cultural condition by exposing them to standards marked by the difference between what was possible then and what is (im)possible now.   (Weimann, 2000, p. 4)

In seeking to determine the 'then' of the cultural context of the making of Shakespeare's plays, theatre and, indeed, Shakespeare, certain themes are particularly germane to our discussion. On the broad canvas, we should consider Shakespeare's society and the emergence of a mercantile/trade-based economy (of course, of particular use when we come to think about the Venice of the play). More specifically we also need to assess the position of Jewish people in the sixteenth century (in England and Venice, although England is all that really concerns us in respect of Shakespeare's work), and the position of women (Portia has always struck me as likely to turn into a Bess of Hardwick [*c.*1527–1608] figure in later life – a remarkable woman who, besides having married four times, was a proto-property magnate and builder of great houses). It will also be important to draw a distinction between the sixteenth century as a period of emergent proto-capitalism (mercantile) in the shift from a land-based economy (Belmont?) and the later high capitalism chosen by directors such as Jonathan Miller and Trevor Nunn in their productions of *The Merchant of Venice* (1969 and 2000 respectively).

The state, religion and the theatre

These three elements all in their different ways interlink with the themes in *The Merchant of Venice*. This section will trace through the context of the 1590s and, at certain points, alert the reader to issues in the play that are intrinsically a part of the making of this period of English history, and which are simultaneously a part of the making of the play.

Elizabeth's reign from 1558 to 1603 has been as much the subject of mythologizing as has the life of Shakespeare. While the period of her reign may be regarded as the culmination of the relative stability established by the Tudor dynasty, Protestant England in the latter half of the century was far from free of threats, surrounded as it was, with Roman Catholic Ireland at its back and faced by the might of Roman Catholic France and Spain. When we remember the origins of the Reformation under Henry VIII, it is hard to see how a clear distinction may be made between the institutions of religion and of politics. In addition to these elements there was the obvious fact that while Elizabeth was monarch, she wasn't a man. Moreover, she didn't seem to have any inclination towards marriage (which, if prudently managed, would have been seen as a move towards legitimizing her reign as well as creating a hoped-for legitimate heir to the throne), although courted by France and Spain. If rumour holds true, Philip II of Spain turned a lascivious and political eye towards Elizabeth, even while he was still married to her sister Mary I. In order to maintain control Elizabeth seems to have achieved this state by means of her own self-iconographic tendencies (as virgin) and the necessity of adopting the persona of a *faux* man, a prince of the realm, as demonstrated in the speech to the troops at Tilbury. William Camden in *The Historie of the Princess Elizabeth* (1630) describes her passage to Tilbury in order to address the troops:

riding about through the ranks of armed men drawn up on both sides her with a leader's truncheon in her hand, sometimes with a martial pace, another while gently like a woman, incredible it is how much she encouraged the hearts of her captains and soldiers by her presence and speech to them.

And in her speech to the troops at Tilbury she is reported as declaring:

> I know I have the body but of a weak and feeble woman, but I have the heart and stomach of a king, and of a king of England too, and think foul scorn that Parma or Spain, or any prince of Europe, should dare to invade the borders of my realm; to which, rather than any dishonour shall grow by me, I myself will take up arms, I myself will be your General, Judge and Rewarder of every one of your virtues in the field. I know, already for your forwardness, you have deserved rewards and crowns; and we do assure you, in the word of a prince, they shall be duly paid to you.   (Quoted in Blakemore Evans, 1987, p. 183)

By way of a postscript, it should also be noted that Elizabeth was an intellectual and an able linguist, qualities not often attributed to the English royal families. Clearly, she was also an astute politician (supported by Walsingham's extensive spy network).

At this point we should pause to reflect on Portia's predicament. First of all, we should note that Portia was, as was Elizabeth, an orphan and a woman of high status alone in a patriarchal society. Productions throughout the decades have developed traditions that portray Portia almost solely in terms of the romantic plot in the play; even her wit as a lawyer is often made manifest through the poetry of the trial scene, more than it is through her deadly, somewhat cruel, logic. There is an often quoted, but possibly apocryphal, feminist question: 'Who is the more powerful, Lady Astor, or the dustman?' The answer given is the dustman because he is male and, no matter the social and material status of the woman, she will always be disempowered in the company of men. This is not because she is somehow 'lacking', but that society is based on an, often covert, patriarchal premise that affords the man automatic status over the woman, despite any disparity in material or intellectual ability in favour of the woman. We can easily transfer this principle to both Queen Elizabeth and Portia. Popular culture has mythologized Elizabeth in many different ways (particularly in Hollywood films and, indeed, in the tourist industry that has sprung up in Stratford-upon-Avon, Shakespeare's birthplace) and made her the centre of a romanticized 'golden age'. However, we may observe in the preceding quotations the need for her, despite the evidence that points to her formidable intellect, to adopt the persona of a *faux* man. Equally Portia, although a privileged and wealthy woman, to say nothing of her intellectual wit, is vulnerable and subject to her father's will and the consequences arising from the choices to be made regarding the caskets. Moreover, we see (and this should become clear in the scene-by-scene analysis in Chapter 6) how she survives the first two suitors by her wit. And, of course, we also witness her intellectual prowess in handling the law, but we also note that in order to accomplish her task, she has to become a *faux* man. These social realities offset the received fairytale Belmont.

When Elizabeth came to the throne many of the ground rules appertaining to the control of the theatre had already been laid under her father Henry's auspices. Of course these rules had been formulated, initially, under the aegis of the Roman Catholic Church, but were later subsumed into that of the Crown with Henry's Act of Supremacy (1534). Control over the theatre also meant the complementary exercise of control over actors and acting through legislation governing the punishment of beggars and vagabonds and, separately, the maintenance of liveried household servants. The classifying of actors along with vagrants and beggars (on the increase in Elizabeth's reign, in part because land enclosures meant that many peasant farmers were forced off their land and had little choice but to travel in search of work, often ending their days as beggars) arose because, prior to the establishing of commercial playhouses in London, and at times afterwards, the players were travellers without permanent homes. It is interesting to note that the building of playhouses marked a significant turning point in modes of commercial exchange. When a travelling company set up their booth stage, the custom was to perform, and then to ask the audience to pay, rather like buskers and street-theatre performers today. However, with the development of the commercial playhouses, the customer was required to pay – according to Thomas Platter, a visitor from Basel, a penny to stand, two pennies to sit, three pennies to sit with a cushion – on entering the theatre before the performance. It should also be noted that entry was by different doors, according to the amount paid, a social, or at least economic, division of the audience that still exists today. The world of the sixteenth century was changing and that change was to do with how business was conducted and how the law – as an ideological formation – was evolving in relationship to commercial exchange.

There was then, as there is today, an interesting relationship between the need for rational law to represent the interests of the community and the freedom required by entrepreneurial commerce. Equally, the same tense relationship exists between the need for the freedom to speak what should be spoken in the theatre, and censorship, at whatever level, to ensure good order. The civil society is also an ordered society. These tensions we may observe in the development of theatre in the emergent commercial society of the sixteenth century, as much as they are revealed in *The Merchant of Venice*. The documents appertaining to the development of theatre are addressed in this chapter, but it is a useful exercise to explore similar elements in *The Merchant of Venice*. For example, the market place, while not the focus of the play, is without doubt one of the driving narrative forces. Shylock, unlike a merchant adventurer such as Antonio (what a thin line divided the roles of Sir Francis Drake as an entrepreneur or a pirate), seems more of a modern man, dealing, as he does, in the financial market place. We may see (in I. iii. 14–24) Shylock at ease in such market-place manners. However, Antonio, as a merchant adventurer not quite as at ease as Shylock in the financial market place, takes the pragmatic view that business is business, and is perfectly prepared to do a deal with the alien whom he has abused regularly on the Rialto (I. iii. 25–177). Commerce, as we know, can move with amazing speed, and sometimes it would appear that the law, as an ideological construct, has difficulty in keeping pace with the changing economic focus. Here we should refer to the trial scene (IV. i. 1–118) wherein the Duke of Venice seems powerless, or unwilling, to intervene in Shylock's demand regarding the bond with Antonio.

Elizabeth had sound political reasons for enacting legislation for the control of theatres and actors; equally, the City Fathers had their reasons for wishing to actually ban theatrical performance. This reveals a distinct ideological difference between the Court and the London mercantile City Fathers that relates to the distinctive issues dividing the spectra of the Reformed churches. In order that we may gain a broader understanding of the tensions between different elements in the society of *The Merchant of Venice*, and by way of example, we will now look at some of the documents and tracts referring to these very issues. Many of the documents also refer implicitly to the growth of an urban society (and the commercial theatre that emerges from it) and the ways by which it impinges on the older agrarian communities, as we see in the implied relationship between Venice and Belmont.

In order to enforce the re-establishment of the (Protestant sounding) Church of England, Elizabeth immediately restored the second prayer book of Edward VI, known as the Book of Common Prayer, and made its use obligatory. That apart, the Act for the Uniformity of Common Prayer and Divine Service in the Church, and the Use of the Sacraments 1559 (to give it its full title) recognized the theatre as a possible site of sedition and riot, because of what may be pronounced on stage, and thus in need of political control:

> And it is ordained and enacted by the authority aforesaid, that if any persons whatsoever, after the said Feast of the Nativity of St John Baptist [24 June] next coming, shall in any Interludes, Plays, Songs, Rhymes, or by other open words, declare or speak anything in derogation, depraving or despising of the same Book or of anything contained therein . . . then every such person, being thereof lawfully convicted in form aforesaid to the Queen . . .   (Blakemore Evans, 1987, p. 57)

The list of penalties varies in severity from a fine of 100 marks for a first offence, through to forfeiture of personal goods and life imprisonment for a third offence. On 16 May the same year (1559) the Queen's second Proclamation against plays was made. In this Proclamation it is clear that while punishment will be exacted on grounds of religious as well as political sedition, there is a move to bring them under a firm level of legal control, rather than exercise an outright ban on theatrical performances:

> the Queen's Majesty doth straightly forbid all manner Interludes to be played, either openly or privately, except the same be notified beforehand and licensed within any city or town corporate by the Mayor or other chief officers of the same; and within any shire, or by two Justices of the Peace inhabiting within that part of the shire where they shall be played. (Wickham, 2000, p. 50)

Any large gathering of common people inevitably led to anxiety on the part of the authorities and, when we consider the devastating effect of diseases such as the bubonic plague (the Black Death), there seems to be every reason to curtail theatrical performances before we even consider the puritan's view that play-acting leads to damnation. On 12 February 1564 there was 'A Precept from the Lord Mayor and Aldermen forbidding the performance of plays'. (We must remember that this is well before the building in 1576 of James Burbage's playhouse, the Theatre, the most noted of the early purpose-built public playhouses, and so must assume that players were still strolling companies performing in whatever 'set-up' [interestingly a term still in current use in the theatre] they could find, whether it be a fair or an inn yard.)

Between the years of the 1560s and the early 1570s, there was a proliferation of Acts, Orders and Precepts all aimed at the control of performances by the travelling players of varying kinds. These and extracts from letters are recorded in *English Professional Theatre, 1530–1660* (Wickham, 2000). However, perhaps the most significant form of legislation appertaining to both the development and the control of the theatres is to be found, curiously, in *An Act for the Punishment of Vagabonds and for the Relief of the Poor and Impotent*, 29 June 1572. There are a number of remarkable aspects to this Act, the first of which is the clear inclusion of players/actors and other entertainers along with the wide variety of the dispossessed of England at the time:

> And for the full expressing what person and persons shall be intended within this branch to be Rogues, Vagabonds, and Sturdy Beggars, to have

and receive the punishment aforesaid for the said lewd manner of life. It is now published and declared and set forth by the Authority of this present Parliament, that all and every such person & persons . . . using subtle, crafty, or unlawful Games or Plays . . . being whole and mighty in body and able to labour, having not Land or Master, nor using any lawful Merchandise, Craft or Mystery whereby he or she doth lawfully get his or her living; and all Fencers, Bearwards, Common Players in Interludes, & Minstrels, not belonging to any Baron of this Realm or towards any other honourable Personage of greater Degree; all Jugglers, Pedlars, Tinkers, and petty Chapmen; which said Fencers, Bearwards, Common Players in Enterludes, Minstrels, Jugglers, Pedlars, Tinkers, and petty Chapmen shall wander abroad, and not have licence of two Justices of the Peace at the least, whereof one to be of the Quorum, when and in what Shire they shall happen to wander . . . shall be taken, adjudged and deemed Rogues, Vagabonds and Sturdy Beggars.   (Wickham, 2000, p. 63)

This act is significant for many reasons over and above the direct effect it had on the theatre of the late sixteenth century. The classifying of theatre people with the motley of the dispossessed of the time, or at least those sections of society perceived and deemed to exist on the margins of tolerance, is still, to an extent, with us today. However we see the situation, the 'lewd manner of life' designated in 1572 has set a certain ambiguity of tone in polite society's attitudes towards theatre workers.

This Act, which was built on earlier acts such as Edward VI's Second Proclamation of 1551, and incidentally, included printers, booksellers and tellers of news as well as players, laid tight restrictions on who may or may not entertain theatrical performance. Glynne Wickham points out that it 'withdraws from the whole squirearchy and gentry up to and including the rank of Baron, their former right to maintain a company of travelling players if they so wished and could afford to do so' (Wickham, 2000, p. 63). Wickham further notes that this does not prevent such companies from performing within their own shire. The implication here is that the restriction is more on travelling than it is on performance. The impetus for the control of theatrical performance is to restrict the granting of royal patents to the notable aristocracy and members of the Court. In 1574 a Royal Patent was issued to Richard Burbage authorizing the

Earl of Leicester's Men to 'use, exercise, and occupy the art and faculty of playing comedies, tragedies, interludes, and stage plays, and other such like as they have already used and studied, or hereafter shall use and study, as well for the recreation of our loving subjects, as for our solace and pleasure when we shall think good to see them' (Wickham, 2000, p. 63). Following on from this early patent, we find the list of names and titles of those personages permitted to have companies formed under their names to be a list of the great and powerful: the Lord Chamberlain's Men; the Admiral's Men; the Queen's Men (later, under James I, the King's Men); the Earl of Pembroke's Men and so on. And while the audiences in the playhouses represented a wide social spectrum, further control was conducted firmly through the institution of the monarchy and down through the offices of the Master of the Revels, to whom all play scripts had to be submitted for approval before a performance could take place.

While the building of James Burbage's playhouse, the Theatre, is often designated the first of the great London playhouses, the Red Lion was the first purpose-built playhouse, in 1567. Nevertheless, the Theatre does seem to mark the rapid development in theatrical building that happened from the mid-1570s on until the early decades of the seventeenth century. This remarkable period of building, writing and playing was not an isolated cultural event. If we think of culture in its all-embracing anthropological sense, as opposed to the restrictive evaluative sense that isolates art from its material and social conditions of making, we then are able to see that this vibrant period of English history is simultaneously the product and producer of the whole level of upheaval that we refer to as 'the early modern age'; an age that encompassed monumental developments in the English language along with, and intrinsic to, the developing national identity, with its mercantile and burgeoning imperial expansion.

The combatants in the debate for and against the theatre in the decades of Shakespeare's professional career were not limited to the Court or City of London authorities. Academics, the literati, satirical pamphleteers, puritan essayists of all descriptions were regular contributors, owing, in part to the rapid growth and access to printing and publishing as well as to the political and religious debates that, with the benefit of historical perspective, we can see were heading inexorably to the English Civil War of the mid-seventeenth century. Less obvious, but nevertheless fascinating, and maybe with fewer axes to grind, were the foreign visitors to London. It does seem to be the case that more and more foreigners were visiting London from other European countries and this, inevitably, must be a significant factor in the emergence of London as an important trading centre intrinsically linked to economic expansion and English world influence in the later decades of the sixteenth century.

Among the many indigenous people engaged in this discourse, for and against, were notable figures such as Philip Stubbes (*The Anatomie of Abuses*, 1583), Thomas Nashe (*Pierce Pennilesse, His Supplication to the Divell*, 1592), Thomas Dekker (*The Gull's Hornbook*, 1609), and Sir Philip Sidney (*A Defence of Poetry*, 1597–80).

From *The Fruits of Playes*, 'Do they not maintain bawdry, infinite foolery, & renew the remembrance of heathen idolatry? . . . where such wanton gestures, such bawdy speeches, such laughing and fleering, such kissing and bussing, such clipping and culling, such winking and glancing of wanton eyes, and the like . . .', or from *Rioting*, 'In a place so civil as this City (*London*) is esteemed, it is more than barbarously rude, to see the shameful disorder and routes that sometime in such public meetings are used' (Nagler, 1952, pp. 128–32), amidst all the pamphlets and essays venting their puritan spleen against the theatre (this is not to say that on occasion they may not have had a point) is Thomas Dekker's *The Gull's Hornbook* (1609), which is a curious mixture of the observation of London life and satiric moral comment, or as E. D. Pendry argues in his 'Introduction' to his edition of Dekker's select writings, 'Here (*The Gull's Hornbook*) and elsewhere Dekker was trying to do something which would seem to him both more difficult and more worthy than mere reportage – constructing his work on a moral plan' (Pendry, 1967). Dekker's writings (not only his plays) are well worth reading in their entirety. Chapter VI of *The Gull's Hornbook* offers advice as to 'How a gallant should behave himself in a playhouse' and, at the very least, gives a witty sense of the 'texture' of the experience of play attendance at one of the children's theatres. The level of satire is sometimes difficult to discern from that of straightforward moral censure:

By sitting on the stage you may with small cost purchase the dear acquaintance of the boys; have a good stool for sixpence; at any time know what particular part any of the infants present; get your match lighted; examine the play-suits' lace, and perhaps win wagers upon laying 'tis copper, etc.   (Pendry, 1967, p. 99)

What is clear from this chapter in *The Gull's Hornbook* is that going to the theatre is a social activity in a very different sense from that of theatre attendance, for the most part, today. We may suppose that one went to the theatre as much to be seen, as to see the play. I have always thought that the real change came when, towards the end of the nineteenth century, electric lighting was employed and the lights were dimmed in the auditorium. It is no accident, surely, that for someone sitting alone (even if you are sitting next to a loved one, you are effectively alone and silent) in the darkened auditorium, watching the dramatic narrative unfold inside the picture frame of the stage, attendance at the theatre became more akin to the act of reading a novel; a uniquely private and individual art activity. This fundamental change in the experience of theatrical performance, from the social to the 'private', coincided with the pre-eminence of the novel as the art form of the nineteenth century.

Philip Stubbes was a prolific writer of the puritan Christian persuasion whose aim was not necessarily to abolish amusements – although at times it is hard to believe that anything but hell fire awaited any participant in the performing and social arts – but only to expose the abuses to be found commonly in these activities. The section *Of Stage-playes and Enterludes, with their Wickednes* (from the first edition of the book, which strikes a more conciliatory tone than later editions) commences with the lines:

All Stage-plays, Interludes and Comedies, are either of divine, or profane matter: If they be of divine matter, then are they most intolerable, or rather sacrilegious, for that the blessed word of GOD, is to be handled, reverently, gravely, and sagely, with veneration to the glorious Majesty of God. . . . Wherefore, whosoever abuseth this word of our GOD on stages in playes and interludes, abuseth the Majesty of GOD in the name. (Freeland, 1973; note, there are no page references in this facsimile edition)

An important feature should be recognized in the opening words of this quotation in which, while attacking the sacrilegious nature of plays dealing in 'divine matter', he also demonstrates a central tenet of Protestantism. The individual's relationship with God is established directly through the (printed) word of God as revealed in the (translated) Bible, and is no longer dependent on the Church as the intermediary between the individual and God.

Stubbes proceeds to address the matter of profane plays, comedies and tragedies. On the question of plays deemed to be profane he declares:

> Beware therefore you masking players, you painted sepulchres, you double dealing ambidexters, be warned betimes, and like good computists cast your accounts before what will be the reward thereof in the end.

Of tragedies he wote: 'But if there were no evil in them, save this, namely, that the arguments of tragedies, is anger, wrath, immunity, cruelty, injury, incest, murder, & such like.' He further stated that as the performers represent gods and goddesses, furies and hags, as such, they will not 'be admitted to the table of the Lord' unless they 'leave off that cursed kind of life, and give themselves to such honest exercises, and godly mysteries, as God hath commanded them in his word to get their livings withall'. And on the matter of comedies his censure was even more extreme.

> Of Comedies, the matter and ground is love, bawdy, cozenage, flattery, whoredom, adultery: the Persons, whores, queens, bawds, scullions, knaves, Courtezans, lecherous old men, amorous young men, with such like of infinite variety: If say there were nothing else, but this, it were sufficient to withdraw a good Christian from the using of them. For so often, as they go to those houses where Players frequent, they go to Venus palace & satan's synagogue to worship devils, & betray Christ Jesus.

The many, and often vehement, attacks from puritan pamphleteers may finally drive us to share the view of Sir Toby Belch in *Twelfth Night* in response to the admonition of Malvolio, the puritan steward of his niece Olivia's household, and ask: 'Dost thou think, because thou art virtuous, there shall be no more cakes and ale?' (II.iii.110–11). Shylock may also be regarded as a somewhat puritanical figure and, interestingly, some of the puritan tracts reveal a respect for the seriousness with which Jews respect their Sabbath and lead abstemious lives (see Philip Stubbes and the *Anatomie of Abuses*). Clearly, Shylock possesses certain of the 'puritanical' traits in his attitudes to Jessica, Launcelot Gobbo and the masquers of Venice (in Act II, scene V).

However, Thomas Nashe in a more satiric mode in the opinions of *Pierce Pennilesse, His Supplication to the Divell* (1592) came to the defence of plays and players, at least those in England:

> To this effect, the policy of plays is very necessary, howsoever some shallow-brained censures (not the deepest searchers into the secrets of government) mightily oppugn them . . . wherein men that are their own masters . . . do wholly bestow themselves upon pleasure, and that pleasure they divide (how virtuously it skills not) either into gameing, following of harlots, drinking, or seeing a play: is it not better (since of four extremes all the world cannot keep them but they will choose one) that they should betake them to the least, which is plays? Nay, but what if I prove to be no extreme: but a rare exercise of virtue?   (Nashe, 1924, p. 86).

Nashe goes on to offer the examples of bravery and virtue as exemplified by the English Chronicles, and notes how it would 'have joyed brave Talbot' (in Shakespeare's *Henry VI*) after being dead some two hundred years, that his triumph should be seen once more upon the stage. And, 'I will defend it against any Collion, or clubfisted Usurer of them all, there is no immortality, can be given a man on earth like unto Plays' (Nashe, 1924, p. 87).

Sir Philip Sidney's *Defence of Poetry* is possibly the best known defence of the poetic arts, of which theatre is intrinsically a part at this point in its development (Van Dorston, 1966). However, we must remember that Sidney died in 1586, the year he wrote the *Defence*, and that it was not published until 1595. The *Defence* is structured under eight main headings: Narration, Proposition, Divisions, Examination I, Examination II, Refutation, Digression and Peroration. The specific reference to drama as poetry falls under the heading of Digression and we may observe immediately that, while the language of drama is regarded as the heightened language of poetry, the material business of theatre is not Sidney's main concern or interest, except to note his disquiet at the seemingly undisciplined quality of contemporary drama. Moreover, Sidney was defending a dramatic form based on the (mis)perceived principles of Aristotle's 'three unities'. The problem with readings of Aristotle on drama is that, while he is describing observed genres in dramatic practice (and anyway in *The Poetics* we only have his students' notes as the extant form of his thinking about tragedy), many interpreters receive his comments as rules for drama. As Peter Thomson has noted, 'The new drama declared its unruliness. The Aristotelian unities of time, action, and place had informed the drama of classical Rome, to which many playwrights looked as a model, but the native narrative tradition proved more powerful in the long run' (Thomson, 2003, p. 51). Sidney in implicitly commenting on the lack of decorum in the 'native tradition', remarks 'how all their plays be neither right tragedies, nor right comedies, mingling kings and clowns'. One interesting feature in Sidney's work is that he makes it clear that we should not mistake a play for real life. 'What child is there that, coming to a play, and seeing *Thebes* written in great letters upon an old door, doth believe that it is Thebes?'

Actors, acting and audiences

Matters of belief and illusion in the theatre have at their centre the function and role of the actor and his/her relationship with the audience, and questions about belief and illusion must be addressed if we are to gain any level of understanding of what happened on the late sixteenth-century stage. As an aside, and by way of an introduction to the problems facing the actor in Shakespeare's plays, I am often reminded of Sidney's *Defence of Poetry* when thinking about the entrance of the players (II.ii) and Hamlet's advice to the players (III.ii) in *Hamlet*. Taking note that central to the many themes of *Hamlet* is a treatise on the matter of theatre and acting with the whole play taking on a metatheatrical aspect, I also have a strong suspicion that

Shakespeare is satirizing Sidney in both Polonius's presentation of the travelling players when they arrive at Elsinore and, to an extent, Hamlet's own advice to the actors. In the first instance, the speeches delivered by the players, as examples of their work, have the ring of an older form of drama about them. Moreover, Polonius aligns himself with Sidney's own fears about the unruliness of the contemporary native drama:

> POLONIUS The best actors in the world, either for tragedy, comedy, history, pastoral, pastorical-comical, historical-pastoral, tragical-historical, tragical-comical-historical-pastoral, scene individable, or poem unlimited. Seneca cannot be too heavy, nor Plautus too light. For the law of writ and the liberty, these are the only men.   (*Hamlet*, II.ii)

Hamlet's advice to the players, 'Speak the speech, I pray you . . . trippingly on the tongue', is often taken by modern interpreters as an indication of the veracity of the various conventions of 'naturalistic' acting methods emanating from the early work of the Russian actor and director Constantin Stanislavski, and the variation that was developed in the United States of America by Lee Strasberg and commonly known as 'The Method'. This line of interpretation is more of an appropriation of Shakespeare's theatre than it is a representation of the conventions of acting being developed at that time. There are two points that may be of use in considering the nature of Hamlet/Shakespeare's advice to the players. Much of what Hamlet has to say consists of an admonition against over-acting: 'Nor do not saw the air too much with your hand. . . . O, it offends me to the soul to hear a robustious, periwig-pated fellow tear a passion to tatters, to very rags. . . . Suit the action to the word, the word to the action, with this special observance: that you o'erstep not the modesty of nature.' The phrase most often referred to is, '. . . was and is to hold, as 'twere, the mirror up to nature'. On the one hand, of course 'over-acting' means overstepping the accepted convention of acting in a particular cultural context, but what it cannot be taken as is the certainty that there is only one true form of acting. What is commonly mistaken as 'truthful' acting is that very particular – and modern –

convention that grew from a quasi-scientific approach to acting in the late nineteenth century. In simple terms the naturalistic acting convention attributed to Stanislavski and, latterly, Strasberg, has achieved a hegemonic status whereby all other conventions are judged (wanting). What is important to remember is that what we term 'naturalistic' or 'illusionistic' acting is but one convention of acting, and one that is not applicable to the poetic drama of the late sixteenth and early seventeenth centuries.

Furthermore, we should consider what holding up a mirror to nature actually means. In eighteenth-century England there was a fashion both for creating landscapes (Capability Brown), and for walking in natural landscapes and then standing with one's back to the scenery and holding a mirror up over the shoulder, and thus framing the landscape: not unlike our modern propensity for endlessly taking holiday snapshots and thus capturing and framing the experience. This process means that we are, effectively, creating nature in our mirrors. When Hamlet advises holding the mirror up to nature, he is, by implication, framing nature. Mirrors do not give an innocent reflection of truth; they frame, and thus construct, a truth that is culturally determined. Theatre that sets out to convince the audience that what is happening on stage is an essentialist 'truth', is really happening, carries with it the seeds of its own contradiction. A drama is a thing of pretence, and some forms of drama are more obviously self-reflexive than others. The language of Shakespeare's plays moves with (self-reflexive) ease between formal poetry, through blank verse, to prose. Thus, we may hear in *Romeo and Juliet* a Petrarchan sonnet spoken by two people, when Romeo and Juliet first encounter each other (I.v.92–105), or the bawdy prose exchanges between the Nurse, Mercutio, and Romeo (II.iv).

The second point contained in Hamlet's advice to the players that is worth considering is the reference he makes to the clowns: 'And let those that play your clowns speak no more than is set down for them'. The 1604 Second Quarto and the 1623 Folio leave the matter there, but the 1603 First Quarto does not. The First Quarto of *Hamlet* may be a rough pirated version of what was performed on the stage of the Globe *circa* 1600, but we do know that it was a performance script, whereas we have no certainty that the 1604 Quarto and 1623

Folio were staged in the published form that has come down to us. The point, however, is that, in the 1603 Quarto, Hamlet goes on to give some examples of the kind of improvisation that he would prefer the clowns not to indulge in. The examples: 'Cannot you stay still I eat my porridge?' and 'You owe me a quarter's wages', and 'My coat wants a cullison', and 'Your beer is sour' presumably would have brought the house down in 1602/3 and may be best understood as comedians' catch phrases of the day (Irace, 1998). Given the popularity and crowd-pulling power of the clowns, such as Will Kemp, in the theatre, the chances of even an established playwright being able to curb the improvisatory excesses of the clown were pretty slim. Launcelot Gobbo in *The Merchant of Venice* while not being one of the most notable clown parts in Shakespeare's repertory, does have what appears to be his own moment of improvisatory excess in V.i.39–48). The excess (or performance potential) of this moment will be examined more closely at the appropriate point in Chapter 6.

Hamlet's speech to the players offers us a number of tantalizing glimpses into the stagecraft of the actors of the time. What starts to emerge is acting in the throes of rapid evolution in much the same way as the crafting of plays was developing. What is also clear is the sense that the forms and conventions of acting were not much to do with the near hegemony attributed to modern psychological conventions of acting.

We should also consider Thomas Heywood's tract *An Apology for Actors* (1612) in our efforts to establish an understanding of what the experience of acting may have involved on the Shakespearean stage (Heywood, 1853, pp. 28–9, 43–4). Heywood seems to follow many of the precepts laid down in Hamlet's advice to the players; his *Apology* adds information regarding the edifying aspect of acting and draws upon classical references to support his argument. While, again, many of his references are related to the art of oratory in the university, he adds action to the list of necessary qualities, such as knowing where to place one's commas, parentheses, breathing spaces and decorum of countenance. He also includes an interesting sentence which is very close to Hamlet/Shakespeare's words: 'It instructs him to fit his phrases to his action, and his action to phrases, and his pronunciation to them both.'

Again, the common interpretation of this guidance is that it enjoins the actor to a form of naturalism in acting; that what happens on stage is 'real'. As Lee Strasberg, the American 'Method' teacher, declared, 'The actor uses real sensation and real behavior. That actual reality is the material of our craft' (Hethmon, 1965, pp. 74–87). Putting aside fundamental questions regarding the nature of reality, we need to ask: What is the nature of the action, and what is the phrase? If the 'phrase' is poetic drama, then the action is suited to that, and *vice versa*. While much is written about the poetry of theatre, more consideration needs to be given to the theatre of poetry.

We may take the performance of a soliloquy as the basis for a fundamental question regarding acting Shakespeare. Should a soliloquy be performed as an internalized monologue? Or should it be performed to the audience; in a sense, putting a question to the audience: 'To be, or not to be – that is the question' (*Hamlet*, Second Quarto, 1604). Or as the First Quarto would have it, even more directly, 'To be, or not to be; ay, there's the point'? Laurence Olivier's 1948 film of *Hamlet* is, perhaps, the epitome of the attempt to perform a soliloquy by Shakespeare as an internalized monologue (Two Cities Film, 1948). In this film the 'To be, or not to be' scene starts with the camera taking us on a labyrinthine journey up a winding staircase, leaving a prone and distraught Ophelia lying at the foot of the stairs. (Given the declared Freudian reading of the play by Olivier, who directed as well as playing Hamlet, we should not be surprised at this labyrinthine journey into Hamlet's mind.) On reaching the battlements we find Hamlet sitting with his back to the camera. The camera zooms in, to the back of Olivier's head, and the soliloquy starts as a voice-over with the audience inside Hamlet's head. Compare this stage/film action with an actor standing on a thrust stage, in the daylight, and surrounded by up to 3,000 people. The material conditions of playing in Shakespeare's theatre surely demanded the playing of a soliloquy as a discourse (even a form of conspiracy) with the audience. The action is suited to the word, and the word to the action.

A commentary on the historical context of *The Merchant of Venice* would be remiss in the extreme if no mention were made of the position of Jewish people in sixteenth-century England. While evidence is slight, certain pointers may be gleaned from various sources, which serve as the basis for a fuller discussion of the play. Philip Stubbes in his *Anatomie of Abuses* appears to adopt a conciliatory attitude towards Jews and their religious practices. He notes in his section on the 'Strict Observation of the Sabbath' that, 'The Jews, are very strict in keeping their Sabbath.' He makes reference to their refusal to prepare food, travel certain miles, and suffer the bodies of malefactors to hang on the gallows on the Sabbath day. He thinks that they overstep the mark, but then contrasts that level of observance with the contemptuous and negligent attitude of many Christians. We cannot know if Stubbes's comments are drawn from direct observation, which would mean that there was a practising Jewish presence and observance in London at the time. What we may assume is a certain level of knowledge and tolerance, at least from the puritan camp, towards Jewish people and certain of their practices.

As we know, the Jews, after a turbulent history in which their fortunes waxed and waned in England, were exiled from England in 1290, in the reign of Edward I. It is likely that their exile was as much provoked by the rise to power of Italian bankers, to whom England gave its patronage, as it was to racism. In 1594 a Portuguese-Jewish physician, Roderigo Lopez, who was actually physician to Queen Elizabeth, was implicated in a series of court intrigues and executed. Although the evidence is inconclusive regarding his involvement in politics, we may assume that the fact that he was Jewish – that is, alien in a society that felt itself surrounded by enemies – was a contributory factor to his demise. It is possible to conceive that an Elizabethan 'Christian' antipathy towards Jews was only matched by a general mistrust of Jesuits or Moors. The point is not to deny the racism, but to argue that anti-Semitism was a part of a broad range of social conventions of prejudice born out of paranoia. It is a matter of historical fact that there were anti-alien riots recorded in London in 1588, 1593 and 1595, and, in a strictly legal sense, Jews were classed as resident aliens (Ward, 1999, p. 128). That many Elizabethans hated Jews, as they hated many other groups of people (and just think of some Protestants and Catholics today), cannot be in doubt. The problem for us, today, is what to do with the play. If it is irredeemably anti-Jewish, what do we do with it? Is the play not populated with outsiders? It that a clue? It is just these questions that we will have to address when we come to discuss further our own possible stage practices and *The Merchant of Venice*.

3 Key Productions and Performances

It is neither desirable nor appropriate in the context of this volume to offer a complete overview of the history of *The Merchant of Venice* in production. However, selected practitioners will be of use because they serve as appropriate cultural signposts by which we may engage with a discourse that, in the different moments of history and context, has been changed by, or has changed, the ways in which we 'read' the play in performance. The criteria by which we approach these mediated forms of the play are not based on any essentialist sense of 'value judgement', but function more as exemplars of how our curiosity may be served in the quest for a fuller understanding of continually shifting values in art. While most of the productions listed below will be employed as reference points, those marked with an asterisk will be the subjects of a fuller discussion. Clearly, any discussion will have to give worthy attention to the matter of Shylock and how he has been represented, his daughter Jessica and occasionally his friend Tubal, who, while being a minor character, may play a significant role depending on how his relationship with Shylock is drawn. Moreover, no account of this play's theatrical life can avoid a reference to the portrayal of Shylock as a comic figure.

With due acknowledgement of the elements of arbitrariness in any selective process, I have chosen to refer to eleven productions in the play's long stage history. Where there is a clearly designated director, his name will be listed first, followed by the actor playing Shylock and then the actor playing Portia, otherwise just the actors playing Shylock and Portia are listed.

* Charles Macklin/Kitty Clive (1741)
* Edmund Kean/Miss Smith (1814)
* Henry Irving/Ellen Terry (1879 and 1880s)
  William Poel/Eleanor Calhoun (1898)
* Theodore Komisarjevsky/Randle Ayrton/Fabia Drake (1932)
  Leopold Jessner/Aharon Meskin/Hanna Rovina (1936)
  Erwin Piscator/Ernst Deutsch/Hilde Krahl (1963)
  Jonathan Miller/Laurence Olivier/Joan Plowright (1969)
  John Barton/David Suchet/Sinead Cusack (1981)
* Bill Alexander/Antony Sher/Deborah Findlay (1987)
  Greg Doran/Philip Voss/Helen Schlesinger (1997)
  Trevor Nunn/Henry Goodman/Derbhle Crotty (2000)

A glance at the stage history of *The Merchant of Venice* will reveal a very mixed view of the play, including a long period when it was recorded as a comedy and then later as a form of social tragedy (Williams, 1979). Equally, we must take account of how the forms of staging are inextricably bound up with changing concepts of scenography as well as the shifts in genre definition. The further back we travel in search of the theatrical mediation of *The Merchant of Venice*, the more we need to understand that the idea of the director as a driving polemical force is a relatively modern phenomenon. So the first three productions in our list do not have designated directors, with the result that the main actor – usually male, usually playing Shylock – is the driving force in creating the performance. In these cases, rather than an external eye choreographing the performance, we find that the performance of the play coalesces around the presence of the major actor, be it Charles Macklin, Edmund Kean or Henry Irving. The play was thought of as a vehicle for an actor, and it was Macklin as Shylock (or Garrick as Lear) that the eighteenth-century audience went to see, and that was the measure by which they judged the production a success, or not. It is an irony of history (or we may say a product of a patriarchal society) that, while the part of Portia is considerably larger than that of Shylock, it is the latter that has commanded attention throughout the eighteenth, nineteenth and twentieth centuries. Even so, the part of Portia has been played by many notable actresses: from Sarah Siddons (1786 and 1803) through

Ellen Terry (1875/79) to Peggy Ashcroft (1932/38), to name but a few amongst the many. This historical study will focus mainly on Shylock, but the proposal in Chapter 6 for the play's performance will give Portia, Jessica and Nerissa their due attention.

We tend to trace the emergence of the director as a significant figure back to George II, Duke of Sax-Meiningen, as *régisseur* assisted by Ludwig Chronegk, in the Meiningen Court Theatre of the 1860s and 1870s. Chronegk, whose task it was to superintend the whole business on stage, would be viewed more as an *über* stage manager than a creative driving force in the production of performance. The emergence of 'polemical' directors has really manifested itself as a phenomenon during the twentieth and twenty-first centuries. By way of an example, we may consider Theodore Komisarjevsky, who directed a startling production of *The Merchant of Venice* for the Shakespeare Memorial Festival Theatre in 1932. Komisarjevsky, who had worked as an assistant to the great post-revolutionary director Meyerhold in the Soviet Union, rejected the cumbersome pictorial settings so common in nineteenth-century British productions of Shakespeare and replaced them with gaily painted deliberately artificial scenes of Venice. The production was visually exciting and clearly influenced by the whole mainland European revolution in the arts that, so often, seems to pass by the inherently conservative arts in Britain. However, its innovatory style was matched by what we, from the perspective of a post-mid-twentieth-century Holocaust, would see as problems regarding the reading of Shylock. Whereas Komisarjevsky's view that the play is a comedy is not necessarily a problem in itself (and is a perspective to be interrogated seriously in our scenic dramaturgical proposal in Chapter 6), the seemingly crude portrayal of Randle Ayrton's Shylock 'as harsh and unsympathetic', and the Prince of Morocco 'as a farcical blackamoor under a red umbrella', would be, at the very least, a pause for concerned reflection. Komisarjevsky's use of *commedia dell'arte* as a stylistic convention is both exciting and fraught with problems (Beauman, 1982, pp. 126–7). *Commedia*, as an improvisatory form of popular performance, has great potential for radically progressive contemporary theatre (as has been demonstrated by the Italian playwright and performer Dario Fo), but could also, so easily, be appropriated to create a grotesque misrepresentation of Jewish and African people in

Shakespeare's plays, as in the Shared Experience Company's production in the early 1980s when Shylock was portrayed as an insect-like Pantalone figure. Nor should this view be taken as an all-encompassing form of ill-thought-out liberalism, as we have also to recognize the potential in all races for sympathetic and unsympathetic actions. What may be open to question in the case of Komisarjevsky's production is the matter of reinforcing racial stereotyping. The polemical director may produce innovatory and exciting imagery in performance, but if this venture is prosecuted without a commensurate concern for the veracity of the text, the end result will be unsatisfactory. Equally, a director who has little regard for the actors and their potential for contributing to the creative process, may have to answer questions regarding his or her own ability to work productively in what, after all, is at its heart a social and collaborative art form.

With a play such as *The Merchant of Venice*, where the play's fame (or notoriety) is derived from one character 'stealing the show', the history of the play in production is marked by the actor playing Shylock, rather than the actor playing Antonio (who is, after all, the merchant of the title). A useful starting point for any discussion on the performance history of *The Merchant of Venice* should be with Charles Macklin in 1741. The history of *The Merchant of Venice*, prior to Charles Macklin's performance as Shylock, is sketchy, and the play does seem to have been both neglected and, in the late seventeenth and early eighteenth century, abused. We may assume that Burbage originally played the role as one of the Lord Chamberlain's men, but little is known except the allusion to Burbage wearing a red wig for the part, 'the red-hair'd Jew'. However, as this reference appeared in a poem entitled *A Funeral Elegy on the death of the famous Actor, Richard Burbage*, that John Payne Collier claimed to have found in an old manuscript, and as Collier has, subsequently, been exposed as a forger, the reference to actors wearing a red wig for the part of Shylock would appear to be without foundation (Lelyveld, 1960, p. 7). The only other possibility is that a tradition may have arisen based on the legend that Judas Iscariot, the betrayer of Christ, was red-haired. Whatever the substance – or lack of it – for this image, the character was treated with scant respect until Macklin took up the challenge in 1741.

The only contemporary adaptation of the play that was received in this period was George Granville's (Lord Lansdowne) adaptation under the title of *The Jew of Venice* that was first performed in 1701. This version followed the trend of the time, which was either to ignore Shakespeare, or, as the 'scholarly' pursuit of men of letters of the time, to adapt the plays to their own sensibilities; the list includes, nearer to Shakespeare, Fletcher's 'answer' to *The Taming of the Shrew* in *The Tamer Tamed*, but less laudable were the assaults of Davenant, Tate, Dryden and Cibber, as well as Granville. Of course, every age has reconstructed Shakespeare's work to its own cultural sensibility; the difference we find in the latter half of the seventeenth century is that the plays were re-written to a greater or lesser extent. The end result was often in the form of song and spectacle imposed on the tragedies and, in the case of Nahum Tate's reworking of *King Lear* (1680/81), the removal of the Fool and a happy ending for Cordelia, who also had an epilogue (delivered by the actress Mrs Barry). A good account of Granville's work on *The Jew of Venice*, which developed the 'romance' between Portia and Bassanio at the expense of the Shylock and Antonio plot, and, in later stagings, allowed Kitty Clive (who also played Portia in Macklin's production) to exploit the part in order to mimic leading lawyers of the day in the trial scene, is given in Toby Lelyveld's book *Shylock on the Stage* (Lelyveld, 1960, p. 23).

Macklin's reputation was built on his ability as a comic actor, so it is a remarkable aspect of theatre history that his performance as Shylock is recorded as having terrified the audiences of the day.

> When he had established his fame in that character, George II went to see him, and the impression he received was so powerful that it deprived him of rest throughout the night. In the morning, the Premier, Sir Robert Walpole, waited on the king, to express his fears that the Commons would oppose a certain measure then in contemplation. 'I wish, your Majesty,' said Sir Robert, 'it was possible to find a recipe for frightening a House of Commons.' 'What do you think', replied the king, 'of sending them to the theatre to see that Irishman play Shylock?'   (Parry, 1891, pp. 67–8)

When Macklin first proposed to revive Shakespeare's play there was a degree of opposition, in part because it was difficult to see Macklin, the player of low comedy parts, undertaking such a 'heavy' role. Then, as now with commercial theatre, the management's collective eye is on the box office takings, more than it is on the creative output. Furthermore, Macklin was obliged, because of the actress's popularity with audiences, to cast Kitty Clive (who was known for her impersonations of pert maids and flighty ladies) as Portia. Macklin's desire to reclaim Shylock from the farcical excesses of Granville's *Jew of Venice* may have been driven by the fact that he was known as an actor who pursued 'the natural' in his performances. This notion of his desire to be 'natural' in his acting may well have had as much to do with his recorded concern with the detail of costuming Shylock as a Venetian Jew, as it was to do with a modern concept of psychological naturalism. When all the odds would seem to have been stacked against the production's success, Macklin's approach to the rehearsal process only added to the general anxiety. Edward Parry wrote:

> The play having been cast, Macklin ordered frequent rehearsals, and doubtless intimated to Fleetwood [the manager of Macklin's theatre] and some of the actors, his intention of playing Shylock as a serious character, though it is said that in actual rehearsal, he merely repeated his lines, and walked through his part without a single look or gesture, and without discovering the business which he had marked out for himself in his interpretation of the Jew.   (Parry, 1891, p. 63)

In performance, however, it was a very different aspect that was offered to the audience. Again, in the *Dramatic Censor* (also published as a 2-volume book in 1770), Francis Gentleman wrote that Macklin:

> looks the part much better than any other person as he plays it. In the level scenes his voice is most happily suited to that sententious gloominess of expression the author intended, which with a sullen solemnity of deportment marks the character strongly. In his malevolence there is a forcible and terrifying ferocity. In the third act scene, where alternate passions reign, he breaks the tones of utterance, and varies his countenance admirably, and in dumb action of the Trial scene he is amazingly descriptive.   (Parry, 1891, p. 67)

Clearly, Macklin's Shylock was, by the theatrical conventions of the day, a radical performance far removed from the *commedia* Pantalone figure of recent decades. Here was a Shylock as the dangerous villain, an interpretation that was to set the mark on the part for many years to come and contribute to the accusation that the play is intrinsically anti-Semitic both in its origins and in its subsequent re-making in theatrical performance. Later, in the scene-by-scene dramaturgical analysis, where the pre-eminent concern will be to address the question: 'How may we perform the play now?', the practice of this volume will be to engage with ways to frame, and thus expose, cultural or politically difficult aspects in the play; this is an imperative common to any dealings we have with plays that come from cultures that seem to be the same as our own, but in fact are very different in outlook and spirit.

Some 73 years later an actor who was socially marginalized and self-marginalizing took the role of Shylock, the villain, the outsider. Edmund Kean, a relatively unknown actor, established his own 'lightning' presence on the stage through, according to the contemporary accounts (Coleridge in particular), the playing of Shylock. Kean's performances were seen and specifically applauded by Coleridge and Byron, but may also be seen as expressing a more general emotional synchronicity with the poetic 'self-justifying self' of the Romantic poets: Shelley and Wordsworth, as well as Byron and Coleridge (Thomson, 2000, p. 122). Indeed Kean's individual physicality of emotion may be said to be entirely in kilter with the poetics of the Romantic Movement. Moreover his later work, particularly his 'feline' performance as Sir Giles Overreach in *A New Way to Pay Old Debts*, may well touch on that wilder edge of Romanticism we know as the (neo-)Gothic.

That Kean delivered a remarkable performance there can be no doubt, but equally we may surmise that he (as did Macklin decades before him) changed, radically, our perception of Shylock. The public expectation of the performance that Kean was to give was as shrouded in uncertainty as was Macklin's. Macklin, even with his lengthy rehearsal period, still gave no hint of the terror he intended to release on stage. Kean, because he only allowed (or the situation at the Drury Lane Theatre only allowed for) a morning's rehearsal on the scheduled day for performance, was equally an unknown quantity.

All expectations were confounded, and William Hazlitt gives a particularly vivid account in his essays on *The Characters of Shakespear's* [*sic*] *Plays*. It is worth quoting.

> When we first went to see Mr Kean in Shylock, we expected to see, what we had been used to see, a decrepit old man, bent with age and ugly with mental deformity, grinning with deadly malice, with the venom of his heart congealed in the expression of his countenance, sullen, morose, gloomy, inflexible, brooding over one idea, that of his hatred, and fixed on one unalterable purpose, that of his revenge. We were disappointed, because we had taken our idea from other actors, not from the play. There is no proof there that Shylock is old, but a single line, 'Bassanio and *old* Shylock stand forth,' – which does not imply that he is infirm with age – and the circumstance that he has a daughter marriageable, which does not imply that he is old at all. It would be too much to say that his body should be made crooked and deformed to answer to his mind, which is bowed down and warped with prejudices and passion. . . . If a man of genius comes once in an age to clear away the rubbish, to make it fruitful and wholesome, they cry, ' 'Tis a bad school: it may be like nature, it may be like Shakespear, but it is not like us.'   (Maclean, 1906, pp. 323–4)

It would seem that Kean's performance not only struck as lightning does, but he achieved dramatic stillness combined with eloquence as no other had before and, further, demonstrated the vocal range of a singer. Toby Lelyveld quotes from William Gardiner attesting to the view that Kean's orotund delivery had 'a range of tones from F below the line to F above it' (Lelyveld, 190, 46–7). Kean's Shylock does seem to have revealed the humanity in the character and, in so doing, moved the perception of Shylock away from the overt 'classical' artifice of John Kemble, and the hating monstrosity of Charles Macklin.

Some sixty-five years later, Henry Irving was to take the next evolutionary step in the staging of the play and the performance of Shylock. The sensibilities of the time, we may assume, allowed Shylock to be transformed from raging tyrant to a man of flawed dignity. In his own book, *Impressions of America*, Irving described Shylock thus:

> I look on Shylock as the type of a persecuted race; almost the only gentleman in the play and the most ill-used. He is a merchant, who trades in the

Rialto, and Bassanio and Antonio are not ashamed to borrow money off him, nor to carry off his daughter. The position of his child is, more or less, a key to his own. She is a friend of Portia. Shylock was well-to-do – a Bible-read man . . . and there is nothing in his language, at any time, that indicates the snuffling usurer.   (Irving, 1884, pp. 265f)

The genesis of Irving's 1879 production of *The Merchant of Venice* seems to have found form during a Mediterranean cruise aboard the yacht of Lady Angela Burdett-Coutts, the granddaughter of the eminent banker Thomas Coutts. According to Barbara Belford in her biography of Bram Stoker, Lady Burdett-Coutts, apart from being a well-known philanthropist and nineteenth-century Irving 'groupie', had many Jewish friends who were, understandably, offended by the way Shylock was caricatured on stage.

Shylock should have the dignity of a man like Sir Moses Montefiore, the philanthropist. At every port, the Levantine Jew drew Irving's attention. Yes, he decided, Shylock should be played as courtly but complex, a man of moods. So obsessed about Shylock was Irving that he refused to finish the trip and was put ashore at Marseilles, where he caught a fast boat-train to London. 'When I saw the Jew in what seemed his own land and in his own dress,' he told Stoker and Loveday at dinner his first night back, 'Shylock became a different creature. I began to understand him; and now I want to play the part – as soon as I can.'   (Belford, 1996, p. 118)

During the course of this voyage Irving visited Venice and various other Italian and Mediterranean cities where he was intrigued by the many different customs, manners, kinds of dress (in Tangier he purchased 'Moorish' costumes to be used in the planned spectacle), and picturesque streets.

We may now assume the two important elements that were to make this *Merchant of Venice* a marked step forward in this play's stage history. While Irving, in the view of many historians, did very little to advance the development of theatre (he hated Ibsen and rejected Shaw), he clearly wanted to take the playing of Shylock beyond the automatically assumed equation between Jew and monster in order that the character's individual complexity as a man might be foregrounded over the stereotyping of 'the Jew'. A factor in focusing the audience's attention on Shylock as an individual with whom we may sympathize, rather than as a type, was the reworking of the received text. Irving's production had two incidents, one of which was Irving's own invention and the other an elaboration. The former was the creation of a scene where Shylock returns to his house after Jessica has eloped with Lorenzo. The elopement scene, with its fantasy of masquers sweeping Jessica and Lorenzo away, was followed by a swift scene change to reveal Shylock as a lonely moonlit figure returning over the bridge to the deserted house. No words were spoken and the brief scene ended with Shylock knocking on the door of his own house. The latter embellishment was Irving's exit after sentence has been passed on him at the end of the trial scene. He seemed distracted, murmuring a few incoherent words as he stared, first at Antonio and then at Gratiano. He stumbled out of the door and the audience heard, off stage, a mob of Christians baying for his blood.

Moreover, Irving's production may be seen as one of the best examples of Victorian pictorial Shakespeare. Of course, while we may argue that this form of pictorial staging is the antithesis of the original social and material conditions of staging Shakespeare, equally we need to understand the cultural context of which this form of staging is intrinsically a part.

It will be worth our while to spend a short time considering the relationship between late nineteenth-century historical narrative painting and pictorial Shakespeare such as was undertaken by Irving. Peter Thomson describes the development of a fascinating relationship between painting and acting in the late eighteenth century, and in particular, the relationship between William Hogarth and David Garrick (the most famous painting on this subject is Hogarth's painting of Garrick as Richard III) (Thomson, 2000, pp. 79–96). Descriptions of Irving's preparations seem to reverse the relationship, and, whereas acting was admitted to the high arts by painters deeming actors and their scenes worthy subjects, theatre makers were now arranging their pictorial scenes on stage in imitation of Victorian historical narrative paintings. In the Royal Albert Museum in Exeter is a painting by James Northcote, RA (1746–1831) of Richard II's entry into London. Clearly this could be a depiction of a scene from a pictorial staging of Shakespeare's *Richard II* as much as a painting in its own right. There is evidence that the theatre makers of the time (scene painters, actor managers) were consciously aiming to reproduce the images of the great narrative paintings on stage. An interesting collision of narrative forms occurs at this point. The narrative of a drama unfolds through a period of time – two timescales in fact: the timescale of the actual hours spent in performance (two hours traffic of the stage, or whatever), and the fictional time covered in the play. These timescales exist irrespective of whether they adhere to some notion of neo-Aristotelian unities, or shifts back and forth in time, or indeed any of the variations on dramatic narrative structure. However, dramatic narrative and time are frozen in such paintings, rather as they are when we detach a single frame from a film reel. Narrative(s) in painting are located in the relationship between the elements of the visual arts: subject, shape, pattern, colour, tone, texture and so on, as well as the cultural narrative that will be created between the observer and the painting itself. Visual imagery is intrinsic to the art of theatre, but unlike a painting, the visual image is one that moves in relation to the unfolding of the dramatic narrative. The narratives of theatrical performance are progressive; the narratives *within* a painting are fixed. But the narratives created by us as spectators and observers of both art forms are in a continuous state of flux.

How does this relate to Irving's production of *The Merchant of Venice*? Percy Fitzgerald offers what appears to be a first-hand account of Irving's work in general, and the production of *The Merchant of Venice* in particular. From the outset, the production was to be visually lavish, drawing its stimulus from the sensory experience Irving had gained on his truncated Mediterranean cruise:

Like some rich Eastern dream, steeped in colours and crowded with exquisite figures of enchantment, the gorgeous vision of the Lyceum pageant seems now to rise in the cold sober daylight. As a view of Venetian life, manners, and scenery, it has never been matched. The figures seemed to have a grace that belonged not to the beings that pace, and declaim upon, the boards. Add the background, the rich exquisite dresses, the truly noble scenery – a revel of colour, yet mellowed – the elegant theatre itself crammed with an audience that even the Lyceum had not witnessed, and it may be conceived what a night it was. The scenery alone would take an essay to itself, and it is hard to say which of the three artists engaged most excelled. . . . The general tone was that of one of Paolo Veronese's pictures – as gorgeous and dazzling as the *mélange* of dappled colour in [a] great Louvre picture.   (Fitzgerald, 1893, pp. 125–41)

Fitzgerald continues at some length extolling the virtues of the pictorial setting before proceeding to describe Irving's Shylock as the genteel Italianized Jew.

a dealer in money, in the country of Lorenzo de' Medicis, where there is an aristocracy of merchants. His eyes are dark and piercing, his face sallow, his hair spare and turning grey . . . in his first scene he is reserved calm and persuasive, without any fiendish emphasis, when his hate escapes him. Even the repeated 'Three thousand ducats? – well!' is reflective rather than hostile. . . . 'The Trial scene' with its shifting passions, would stamp Irving as a fine actor . . . how different from the conventional violent hatred! Instead, his explanation is given with true and respectful dignity, not a threat; and when he further declares that it 'is his humour', there is a candour, which might commend his case, though he cannot restrain a gloating look at his prey.   (Fitzgerald, 1893, p. 135)

Irving's portrayal of Shylock, we may suppose inevitably, gave rise to a great deal of controversy, with conservative theatregoers finding too radical the idea that Shylock was a dignified and cultivated man; a view that inevitably gives rise to the suspicion that maybe it is the attitudes and behaviour of the Christians which could bear closer scrutiny.

While there is an implicit admission that Shylock, throughout the decades, has stolen both the play and the show, mention must be made of Ellen Terry's performance of Portia, through a number of different productions: first of all with Squire Bancroft and Marie Wilton at the Prince of Wales theatre, but later, to great acclaim, forming an electrifying collaboration as Portia to Henry Irving's Shylock. It is worth recording some of Ellen Terry's responses to playing Portia as recorded in one of the lectures on Shakespeare she gave towards the end of her career. Irving gave Terry a fuller run at the part than had hitherto been afforded to many actors playing Portia, by keeping Act V and the comedic ending in Belmont. (It is a misnomer to assume in theatrical history that Irving cut the fifth act so as to afford Shylock/Irving the grand and final exit. The fifth act was cut, but only for two months or so when a one-act play called *Iolanthe* was substituted.) Terry pointed out in her lectures that there was an inconsistency in, on the one hand, Irving portraying Shylock as a man suffering and wronged, and on the other, Portia as a noble creature, when of course Portia is also one of Shylock's oppressors. Portia preaches mercy, but shows little in the end. Terry makes it quite clear that she was uneasy over the harsh way in which Portia entraps Shylock. Moreover, Terry's Portia was ambiguous in her attitude towards Bassanio, as we might guess when Portia becomes an intelligent, astute character in the hands of an actor of Terry's ability. She viewed Bassanio as a layabout who lives by his charm. However, these contradictions were voiced only in the lectures, and contemporary accounts record that on stage, Shylock was tragic and Portia noble.

On 9 May 1987, Christopher Edwards wrote in the *Spectator* of Bill Alexander's production of *The Merchant of Venice*:

> Of all Shakespeare's plays this one probably troubles the modern conscience the most; anti-Semitism is so uncompromisingly expressed by many of the characters and colours the entire mood of the work. It ought not to be performed – one has often heard that argument, even if it is rare for anyone to actually accuse the playwright of holding anti-Semitic views.

Nevertheless, particularly in our post-Holocaust world, the imputation remains that the character of Shylock, what he does, and what is done to him in the play, are read in the light of contemporary political sensibilities. Any contemporary actor or director, or for that matter teacher or critic, cannot afford to ignore the underlying issues of the play. The question remains: What should we do with Shylock's relationship with the Christian mercantile world of Venice?

Alan Sinfield wrote an essay entitled 'Four Ways with a

Reactionary Text', the purpose of which was to consider the options available when we are confronted by a text that, in some way, presents an ethical problem to contemporary sensibilities (Sinfield, 1983, pp. 81–95). He starts with the premise that all 'Books [and of course for us performances] promote versions of relationships between people, and, usually they deploy powerful naturalizing strategies which suggest that the people presented and the things they do are both true and inevitable', and furthermore, as has already been argued earlier in this volume, we need to consider what version of reality is being promoted. No idea could be more apposite to the study and experience of Shakespeare's plays in performance, where the social and cultural contexts are pre-eminent factors in deciding the individual play's 'reality'. Among the options that Sinfield argues are available to us is the proposal of 'deflection into form(alism)'. In this he quotes Terry Eagleton's suggestion that 'our aim should be to abolish literary criticism and revive rhetoric in its place, that is, a study of the ways in which discourse works upon and produces ideology, the social relations within which it is produced and received, its articulation with other discursive and non-discursive practices' (Sinfield, 1983, pp. 86–7). Moreover, in theatrical practice (I would add), we must take account of the discourses between the actor and the text/script, and the discourses that may arise between the actor(s) and the spectators.

Taking due account of all that has been stated in the preceding paragraph, the next section of this chapter records the views of a Jewish actor who has played Shylock. Sir Antony Sher is, without doubt, one of our leading actors in Shakespeare's plays, but one whose range of playing also extends to a wide variety of contemporary works. He has even something of the Renaissance polymath about him: actor, playwright, novelist, autobiographer, and painter. Sher is South African by birth, but took British nationality some years ago, and the culturally complex mix of being South African, Jewish and gay places him in a dynamic relationship with the issues that arise from *The Merchant of Venice*. In the course of the conversation, we refer to Gregory Doran, one of our leading and most articulate contemporary directors of Shakespeare's plays. Doran is Sher's life partner as well as a professional collaborator in the production of theatre.

Conversation with Sir Antony Sher on playing Shylock and on contemporary stage productions of *The Merchant of Venice* with particular reference to the 1987 Royal Shakespeare Company production. Director: Bill Alexander; Shylock: Antony Sher; Portia: Deborah Findlay; Antonio: John Carlisle; Bassanio: Nicholas Farrell

C.M.   What questions did you feel needed to be asked for you, a Jewish actor, to be able to play Shylock now?

A.S.   This wasn't remotely a problem for me, because as soon as we started work on the production, what was very clear to me from the outset was that playing Shylock the Jew corresponded to a political contradiction that obsesses me still; and obsession is not too strong a word. It is the syndrome of the persecuted turning into the persecutor. To some extent, while the sense of this political contradiction comes from my South African background, it is also something that I was party to, albeit unconsciously. When I left South Africa and came to London, I tried to untangle this terrible thing that I'd been part of, this atrocity that I'd lived through without noticing. I had to ask myself the question, how was it that my family, who had fled anti-semitic persecution in Eastern Europe, how could they have conceivably become people who voted for the Nationalist government in South Africa? How could they, in a very middle-of-the-road way, support apartheid?

In trying to untangle this internal contradiction it became apparent to me that it is actually a very human state of affairs that is applicable to many of us to a greater or lesser extent. It is not a particularly nice one, but it is one that does occur again and again. We may think of Jews coming from Eastern Europe to South Africa and apartheid; the Afrikaners themselves, they who had been the losers and the victims of the Boer War (the war in which the British invented concentration camps), turn into the Afrikaners of apartheid; Robert Mugabe, a victim of colonization, turns into the monster that he is now; Israel, the children of the Holocaust, turn into the terribly violent, aggressive, unsympathetic Israelis of today.

So Shylock seems to me to stand as a representative of that very human syndrome and it seems to me to be a type of role that has arisen for me quite a lot as an actor. My real concern in playing Shylock was that we needed to show, perhaps in a stronger way than Shakespeare's words alone do for our society, the society that Shylock lives in and what it is like for him. I think if you can really gain a feeling for that social milieu, that cultural texture, you are well on the way to confronting the problems the play presents to our post-Holocaust society.

Once we decided to set the play in Renaissance Venice, I read quite a lot about the ghetto in Venice and the fact that there were a lot of Turkish Jews living there at that time. I was concerned to find a way of me playing it that was not going to be Jewish in a sort of shoulder-shrugging way, or with a Petticoat Lane accent. I needed to find something that was right for both the production and me. The solution was finding out about this big Turkish population in the ghetto, because somehow one could allow his whole physicality to go through a much older route rather than the more clichéd representations of Shylock the Jew.

C.M.   One impression that comes through clearly is the way you play him as a more Levantine or Sephardic Jew. One of the broadsheet critics writes about you playing him as a Sephardic Jew, which I think is quite interesting particularly when we are thinking about the actions of present-day Israel. I had a Syrian research student working with me who held the view that the Sephardic Jews, who had lived peacefully alongside the Palestinian Arabs for generations, were his cousins and were as equally oppressed by the current activities of the Israeli government as the Palestinian Arabs. The evidence I have gleaned from reading newspaper reviews of your performance demonstrates that your performance, by dwelling on the character and image of an 'Eastern' Jew, raised the kind of awareness and complexity that we are talking about.

A.S.   And as I said, that choice was mostly about trying to find a way of him not being a clichéd 'European' Jew. Because the physicality of parts is very important to me as an actor, I had to be able to express him physically, yet I was also terrified of slipping into any of the clichés.

It is interesting to note how different actors approach acting. Clearly, the physicality of roles was something that Laurence Olivier was also concerned with. What is interesting about the production of *The Merchant of Venice* in which Olivier played Shylock is that he is not Jewish, but he did have a Jewish Director in Jonathan Miller. They decided on Shylock as a kind of Disraeli figure, whom I remember well as I saw the production several times. I have to admit that I found the production rather frustrating in that Olivier played so much against the Jewishness of Shylock that he had gone out the other end and could well have been playing one of the Christians. The idea was obviously that this man was highly assimilated into the Christian Venetian mercantile culture.

Anyway, to go back to the idea of creating the right society, through the rehearsals, and eventually the performances, we made life very tough for Shylock whenever we could. You know, for instance, there are references in the text to Shylock being spat at and we literally did that as much as we could. It was an extremely unpleasant experience with various actors' saliva lodging in this huge beard that I had grown for the part. By the end of the run, I had got to know everyone's saliva very well, particularly that of the smokers in the cast. Seriously, I do believe that this level of physicality was necessary for the way we wished to present Shylock. Another instance of the physicality of playing was in the scene where Shylock discovers that his daughter Jessica has gone, and which ends with him and Tubal. We began that scene very violently with the 'Salads' [a common theatrical nickname for the two characters Salerio and Solanio] and their barbaric behaviour, which, we suggest, provides him with the motive – we might say need – to carry through with the bond. You would need to understand that journey as being central to our production and I'm quite proud of us doing that; treating the violence towards Shylock in that way. So, the simple answer to your question is that I didn't have the remotest problem as a Jew playing Shylock, although some time I'd like to talk about whether only Jews should play Shylock.

C.M.   And whether only black people should play Othello, do you think?

A.S.   I don't think that can be so in either case. Why am I as an actor allowed to adopt somebody else's nationality, accents, sexuality? A necessary consequence of my profession is that I continually have to be things that I am not. That I can adopt another man's soul, but I can't adopt his skin colour, seems absurd to me. That kind of specificity with regard to ethnicity is probably a phase we have already gone through, as now black actors increasingly play Henry V at the National [Theatre] or whatever; the hope is that eventually we will become colour blind to the extent that again white actors will play Othello. Similarly, it would be absurd if only Jews played Shylock. If you are a good enough actor to be able to enter into another man's soul, then one should be able to play their ethnicity, which is what I think the great actors can do.

C.M.   How did Portia work out in your production? Some of the reviews that I've read, to quote, state: 'What do you do with a heroine who delivers a pretty pious speech about justice and then uses a cheap trick to win her court case.' Is she both élitist and racist as some reviewers perceived her to be in Bill Alexander's production?

A.S.   I think that whole side of the play is a big problem for me. Once, when I felt that we had fairly successfully solved our side of the play, in other words the Shylock story, you then realize that there is another side, a considerable side, which is so incompatible with the Shylock narrative. The contrast is even more noted if you aim to make the Shylock narrative as hard and harsh and cruel and as uncompromising as we did. I think this romantic fairy tale running alongside becomes almost impossibly difficult. I think you can live with it in the early part of the play because there is a certain cruelty in the caskets and there's a dark side to Bassanio and Antonio's unfulfilled gay relationship, but matters become impossible when you get to Act Five and Shylock is finished, and you have then got to be concerned about silly arguments about rings. We performed the play for about two years with the old RSC cycle of a year in Stratford and a year in London. I began that whole process by believing that we had made the play work and I ended it by believing that we hadn't, and that it was impossible to make the play work; that time had turned that play into one of the ones that no longer work.

C.M.   One of the plays that university students will often argue cannot be played now is *The Taming of the Shrew*.

A.S.   If anyone believed that, which I did, they needed to see Greg's current production of *The Taming of the Shrew* where I believe he has proved me wrong. He started out thinking that the solution to the problem was to be found in framing Shakespeare's play with John Fletcher's play *The Tamer Tamed* in a double bill. In the end he decided that the key to the play's reception now has to be in Shakespeare and particularly in the Katerina/Petruchio narrative, and he made this work so well that it didn't really need Fletcher or anyone else to 'answer' Shakespeare's play or make any excuses for it.

C.M.   The other prominent question in my mind in *The Merchant of Venice* is the matter of Bassanio's and Antonio's sexuality and the nature of their relationship. While sodomy could incur the most horrible torture and death in the sixteenth and seventeenth centuries, there was no clear distinction in male friendships, as there seems to be now, between hetero- and homosexuality. What kind of friendship is it? Such friendships, it would seem, physical or not, between older and younger men could be very close and generally accepted.

A.S.   Greg would be interested in this theme because, when he was still an actor, he and Michael Cadman played the 'Salads' as a gay couple in our 1987 production. There was a kiss between them suggesting that it was a society where you could be gay, but the older generation – Antonio's generation – would have a problem with that. Recently I was looking at some material about Leonardo da Vinci and Michelangelo. There, of course, again you have a society in Renaissance Italy (did you know the day we assume Shakespeare was born on was also the day that Michelangelo died, talk about passing on genius!) where homosexuality was tolerated – as long as you were discreet. But both Leonardo and Michelangelo, coming from very different points of view, found it completely impossible to put into practice. Michelangelo because he was so influenced by Savonarola, who would clearly burn you at the stake for the mere pat of his bum, and Leonardo perhaps because he was arrested for sodomy as a young man, and although the charge was dropped through lack of evidence, got a terrible fright and for the rest of his life spoke about sex as something to be resisted.

I am drawn back to being able to play another man's soul. If you are playing something, somebody, that is out of your experience you need to immerse yourself as far as is possible in order to achieve a necessary degree of empathy with the experience or the person. When I played Macbeth, I met with two real-life murderers in order to discuss their experiences. I wanted to go into as much detail that they would tell, or that I could bear, of what that experience is like. There is much about the Lee Strasberg American Method in acting that I like and admire and, when well used, it produces wonderful results. However, we need to approach it with caution for, like any tool, it can be misused and easily satirized. In the end I use what I need and adopt what seems to me to be most appropriate for the purpose. It is part of how I work in order to achieve integrity with the human being I am portraying. I have found with certain roles, during the course of the evening I have to stay inside it, which people might call method acting. What I mean by this is that I cannot always be social with other people in the dressing room before the show. Some parts demand that you start the creation of the character some time before you walk on stage. This is something that Sello is certainly doing at the moment with Othello [Sello Maake Ka

Ncube is a South African actor who was playing Othello with Antony Sher as Iago at the time of this interview].

C.M.   You say that when you were rehearsing Shylock you were cut off from the whole Belmont, Bassanio and Portia narrative. How do you then cope with working together when you come to the Trial Scene?

A.S.   I should say that it is only in the early rehearsals that you are separated, just by the practicality of the production and the director's working methods organizing the directing of your scenes and then their scenes. Later on, when you start doing run-throughs and so on, you will see one another's work. However, by then most of the most important discussions and decisions will have taken place in private early on in rehearsals, so you will only be seeing a sort of semi-finished result. Even then you are not best placed to judge how the production is holding together because you are often – and this is back to the idea of the Method – inside your character; even though you might watch a scene between your own scenes, you will have your mind full of what you have just done and what you are about to do. There is no way that you can be like an objective audience saying, 'Oh, that's interesting what they've done with Belmont.' It is often interesting for actors, when their production is filmed or televised, which they seem to do more and more now by putting a few cameras around the auditorium and film every couple of performances, that you finally get to see the production in the way that relates to how an audience saw it.

C.M.   Curiously, there are very few films of *The Merchant of Venice*. About thirteen I think, but they are mostly silent movie extracts from the play, or extracts filmed for educational purposes. There are two full videos, which were made from the Jonathan Miller production in 1969, and the Trevor Nunn production of 2000.

A.S.   Although I think that a film could solve my big problem with Act Five of *The Merchant of Venice*, in that you could keep cutting back to Shylock perhaps, with this sentence that is looming over him. That would create an interesting silent commentary on the whole Belmont business of Act Five. It will be interesting to see what they do in this forthcoming film of *The Merchant of Venice* with Al Pacino as Shylock.

C.M.   I remember in a previous conversation we had when Greg was present that you asked why we couldn't just cut Act Five. Greg disagreed.

A.S.   This is, in part, an example of a discussion between a purist and a non-purist. Greg would never dream of cutting any part of Shakespeare, he loves it so much and believes that one should try and make the whole received text work. You have to understand that I was speaking heresy at that moment! I have to say that I find Act Five so silly and trivial after the very ugly and very human events that have been happening to Shylock, to suddenly start being concerned about missing rings. It is so disproportionately trivial to have that as the end to the play. Contemporary directors and actors try to get around this in different ways; I think Trevor Nunn made Jessica carry on the Shylock story to the extent that you realize that she and Lorenzo are not going to be happy and that she is awkward with these Christians.

C.M.   I seem to remember a nice point in Jonathan Miller's 1969 production when everyone, bar Antonio and Jessica, have gone into the house at the end of Act Five. They are left alone on the stage facing each other, realizing that they are the two outsiders.

A.S.   They can be the two awkward elements in this ménage. Jessica is still Jewish and Antonio has possibly lost the love of his life. You could, of course, play Act Five in *Merchant* as all the Belmont crowd being very selfish, unsympathetic, just horrible rich brats, but that would be so alienating.

C.M.   And Greg in his 1997 production did seem to portray Portia as a rich, self-obsessed and fairly brutal person; it came out clearly, for example, in her dismissal of the Prince of Morocco, and her habit of cuffing the servants around the head.

A.S.   Mind you, all that line of thinking might just fit in with my sense that, while it is Shylock's play, he needs Venetian/Belmont society to measure against and be measured. The trouble is that when you've played him, you want it to be about him and I would still argue that, emotionally, the audience's main interest is in Shylock's side of the events. There is a deep irony in that Shylock, like Othello, is indispensable to that society, but if they once transgress . . .

As an addendum to this dialogue, I think that it is well worth recording the reference to his performance as Shylock in Sher's autobiography, *Beside Myself* (Sher, 2002). It was on the occasion of the annual celebrations for Shakespeare's 'birthday' that the then company wished to demonstrate against the invitation to the South African Nationalist ambassadorial representative to take part in the celebrations. They were denied permission to make a statement from the stage, but . . .

> I [Antony Sher] found out where the man was sitting. Stalls, middle of row B. Good. When we got to the trial scene and Shylock's speech to the court –
>
>> You have among you many a purchased slave
>> Which like your asses, and your dogs and mules
>> You use in abject and in slavish parts . . .
>
> – I took hold of one of the court attendants, played by the Coloured [*sic*] actor Akim Mogaji, led him to the front of the stage, pointed directly at the South African and unleashed Shylock's venom, and ours, the company's, straight at him.   (Sher, 2002, pp. 192–3)

4 The Play on Screen

There are in the region of thirteen film adaptations of *The Merchant of Venice*, with the earliest (1908) being an American silent film with William V. Ranous as Shylock and Julia Swayne-Gordon as Portia. However, the problem is that many of them are filmed excerpts of the play and not, in any significant way, efforts to re-present the play through the medium of film. The BBC produced the earliest television version in 1947, with Abraham Sofaer as Shylock and Margaretta Scott as Portia, which was followed by an Italian film in 1952 and three television productions in 1955, 1972 and 1980 (Davies and Wells, 1994, pp. 18–49). Two theatrical productions, one directed by Jonathan Miller with Laurence Olivier as Shylock and Joan Plowright as Portia (1969), and the other by Trevor Nunn with Henry Goodman as Shylock and Derbhle Crotty as Portia (2000), were subsequently reproduced as video recordings and will serve as examples for our analysis. There are two other video productions of the play that are readily available. They are: Cedric Messina – director; Frank Finlay – Shylock; Maggie Smith – Portia (BBC, 1972); and Jack Gold – director; Warren Mitchell – Shylock; Gemma Jones – Portia (BBC/Time Life, 1980). Both television productions suffered the fate of many televised productions of the time in that they are generally regarded as anodyne attempts to place the entire canon on televisual record. Warren Mitchell's casting as Shylock should have been important if only for the fact that it offers the example of a Jewish actor playing the part. However, Mitchell presents Shylock in precisely the manner that Antony Sher sought to avoid – 'the stage Yid' – and the serious attempt to deal with anti-Semitism is dissipated.

Clearly, the mediation of *The Merchant of Venice* through the electronic media has more often been undertaken through television (live and video recording) than it has through film. (Although, as this volume is being written, a film version has been released in the United States of America with Al Pacino playing Shylock.) This chapter, however, will focus on the nature of television as a medium for the dissemination of Shakespeare.

> television is a universal medium to a far greater extent than the theatre or even literacy: as an oral and visual form it is accessible even to the unlettered, its complex visual dialect easier to learn than spoken or written language. It therefore can claim, more than any other cultural form, to be a national communications medium, the primary system of an authentically 'national' culture. More so than print (even popular newspapers), certainly more than other 'cultural' discourses such as literature and theatre, television has succeeded in incorporating itself into the rhythms of social life, so that the medium has become a normal part of everyday experience.   (Holderness, 2002, pp. 30–1)

It is in this sense that television has been claimed as having more right to be recognized as a 'national theatre' than the building and company sited on the South Bank of the Thames in London. The history of the production of Shakespeare and many other plays of the western canon on television in the United Kingdom stretches back to the late 1930s. On this evidence we may claim that more people have had access to Shakespeare's plays on television than in any of the playhouses in postwar Britain.

The case for the appropriateness of Shakespeare on television has scholarly support. Terry Hawkes, for example, proposes that television as a medium is a successor to the social experience of theatre attendance in the Elizabethan public playhouse. He argues that both the Elizabethan theatre and television offer the possibility of a social activity, rather than, ironically, the solitary experience of contemporary theatre-going (Hawkes, 1985). Both the former encourage(d) simultaneous response and discussion, whereas the experience of attending the theatre today is usually more akin to the experience of reading a novel: we sit in the dark, isolated from all those around us, in enforced silence as the incontestable narrative unfolds before us.

The Merchant of Venice is a play that lends itself readily to presentations that site their performance in what may be described as 'social interiority'. I employ the term 'social interiority' in this context to mean a dramatic locus where the emphasis is placed on understanding the social relationships and interactions of characters represented, rather than on the interiority and interaction of individual character or psyche. 'Interiority' forms a part of the phrase so that we may distinguish a more domestic form of social interaction from situations that present a broader, or even epic, canvas. In *The Merchant of Venice* the lives of the characters do not really step outside the social interiors of business contracts, the inextricably linking of marriage with commodities, and the legal system. In this play there is no room for the flights of fancy or fantastical disguises that create confusions that will need to be resolved – happily for the most part. Traditionally, we have identified the two worlds of the play as representing two contrasting elements: Venice/mercantile; Belmont/pastoral. This contrast is, of course, a perfectly justifiable one, but when alternative ways of perceiving the two societies of the play are presented, our curiosity must be aroused. Just such an instance is presented in two television adaptations from original stage performances. Both stage presentations (coincidentally both from the Royal National Theatre, although the Miller/Olivier production was in the Old Vic Theatre in the very early days, before the South Bank complex was completed) emphasize what I have chosen to describe as 'social interiority', and, while the earlier production certainly sees Belmont as 'stately home rural' (there are exterior location shots), it does not possess quite the harmony we expect in the resolution of the pastoral. In the later production, by Trevor Nunn, even the streets of Venice seem to be indoors, and Belmont could be in Torquay or, if we wish to be more cosmopolitan, St Moritz! The social interiority of Nunn's Venice veers from seedy nightclubs more fitting for early 1930s Berlin (the production is set in that period) to the ghettos of Warsaw, and Belmont is manifested as a projection of its passionate but prickly mistress, and is far from a being a restful pastoral retreat wherein all ills are healed.

Antonio's opening lines to the play,

> In sooth I know not why I am so sad,
> It wearies me, you say it wearies you:

But how I caught it, found it, or came by it,
What stuff 'tis made of, whereof it is born,
I am to learn: and such want-wit sadness makes of me,
That I have much ado to know myself.

                                                    (I.i.1–6)

could well have been the inspiration of the beginning and ending of
both Miller's and Nunn's productions. Antonio's first speech of the
play sets the tone for both performances. Similarly, with both
endings Belmont fails, it would seem, in bringing very little general
happiness, or for that matter any confidence of resolution. This
avoidance of a comedic ending where all things proper find their true
place may well be the appropriate *fin de siècle* outcome for the late
twentieth century when we strove (and still strive in the twenty-first
century) to avoid explicit and implicit anti-Semitism. Whatever our
political reading, both productions leave us with, at the very least, a
deep sense of unease emanating from the playing of Jessica at the
play's end. In the Miller production both Antonio and Jessica are left
as outsiders, with Antonio recognizing that he has lost his 'lover' and
Jessica having lost her heritage – for what? – a less than trustworthy
character in Lorenzo. For Nunn, Jessica's Hebrew lament, *Eshet Chayil*
(*A Woman of Virtue*), on receipt of the news that Shylock's estate
would fall to her husband, seals the growing tension that has built
since the awkwardness created by Portia's mock sense of betrayal
through the trick of the rings (Edleman, 2002, pp. 265–6).

   Jonathan Miller's production sets the play in the period of 'high
capitalism' of the late nineteenth century. The claustrophobic atmosphere created by the crowded interior design of the 'Victorians', with
their heavy furniture and accumulated bric-a-brac, serves to emphasize what I refer to as 'social interiority'. Inevitably there is a fair
degree of editing of the extant text with the aim of removing as much
of the comedic element as possible, as is evidenced by the almost
total exclusion of the clown Launcelot Gobbo and Old Gobbo (his
father).

   The emphasis in Miller's production is on money, with the
contract at the centre as, it seems, a driving force in determining the
nature of all relationships. This fiscal theme is intrinsically bound up

with Miller's project, as it is with that of many modern directors, to address the problem of anti-Semitism. Miller's intention was to enforce the idea that modern anti-Semitism relates to nineteenth-century capitalism more than it does to Christians placing the blame for the death of Christ on the Jewish nation (Ansorge, 1970, p. 53). The Bassanio/Portia relationship, with a forty-year-old actor wooing a forty-four-year-old actress, as well as lacking any potential passion, reinforces the notion that Bassanio is in it for the money (not that we gain any sense of intimacy in his relationship with Antonio as an alternative relationship). Even more mercenary seems the Lorenzo and Jessica relationship on the part of Lorenzo, whose sole motive seems to be financial. But so ineffective is the character in this production that one has the suspicion that he won't be able to put the money to any useful purpose. Jessica's reception at Belmont is less than warm, with Portia at her most dismissive. She even forgets, or feigns to forget, Jessica's name at one point, such is her lack of regard for the young woman who has risked all.

The trial-scene setting is suggestive of attendance at a board meeting of international bankers. The characters are grouped around a table over which the 'business' is transacted in what may be described as an atmosphere more of intellectual calm than of emotional intensity. At a cursory glance, Olivier's assimilated Jew – at least in appearance and general demeanour – is indistinguishable from the assembled Christian 'bankers'. Because of this atmosphere of seeming control, intensified by Portia's cold handling of the punishment meted out to Shylock, Olivier/Shylock's collapse in the final moments is all the more disturbing. It is at that point that we – actors and audience – are all complicit in Shylock's demise. It is clear from the glances that pass between the characters that they realize the enormity of what they have done.

The mood of nearly all the characters is recovered by the time we reach Belmont. However, in contrast, a hollow ring is noted in Lorenzo's relationship with Jessica. 'In such a night as this . . .' and the lines that follow, rather than being expressions of love, seem not to carry any sense of truthfulness. We may sense a less than happy ending. A notable moment of this television production comes when Jessica is left alone, alienated by the Christian terms of her father's will, after all the others have gone inside. In the television adaptation, Antonio is the last to leave her alone. In the stage production, he stays with Jessica when all the rest have gone, perhaps recognizing that both of them are, in their different ways, the outsiders to this play's 'happy' conclusion.

Personal and social dysfunction seems to lie at the heart of Trevor Nunn's production, with Antonio's first speech leading the mood of the play to an even greater extent than in Miller's production. Whereas the melancholy demonstrated by Jacques in *As You Like It* may be put down to the 'playing' out of a self-knowing affectation, Antonio's in *The Merchant of Venice* seems to signal a genuine disorder of his humours, his 'green sickness', which would suggest, according to the sixteenth-century theory of the bodily humours, that Antonio was suffering from love-sickness. The playing of Antonio by David Bamber (incidentally with a Mancunian accent, which distanced him from the other Christians of Venice with their decidedly 'cut-glass' accents) presented us with an inwardly troubled and alienated man, and one with whom, in this production, I have never found much empathy. Antonio, the 'merchant' of the play, remains a troubled but passive lack of presence, 'the absent centre around which the action of the comedy revolves' (Ryan, 2002, p. 21), whereas Henry Goodman's Shylock, equally inwardly troubled, grows in stature throughout the film and is a far more complex character than that presented by Olivier.

Shylock's first meeting with Bassanio seems a reasonably civilized affair, but when Antonio enters, the mood changes markedly with displays of real animosity between Shylock and Antonio. This may be read as an attempt to circumvent the general anti-Semitism of the Venetians towards the Jews, suggesting that Shylock and Bassanio behave reasonably well to each other. If this is the case, it is quickly subverted by Antonio's entrance, with Shylock performing his speech, 'How like a fawning publican he looks!' (I.iii.36–47), directly to the camera and thus addressing us, his audience. It is an interesting tactic used also by Launcelot Gobbo in this production, one which demonstrates how the 'fourth wall' of the television screen may be broken through. Direct address of this kind had been used to remarkable effect in Jane Howell's television directing of the *Henry VI* trilogy in the BBC/Time Life production (1983). Shylock's complexity and inner turmoil in Nunn's production is demonstrated aptly in his extended scene with Jessica (Act II, scene iv) as he is about to depart to dine with Antonio and Bassanio. Their early moments reveal a tenderness that, in its overwhelming closeness, signals a degree of unease which is centred on Shylock's love of Jessica's (dead) mother. The Hebrew lament *Eshet Chayil*, part of which we have noted is repeated by Jessica at the end of Act V, is performed between them with an intensity that serves only to reinforce the seeming interdependence created by their social isolation, which, in its turn, reveals their social interiority. However, as Shylock hears of the carnival that is to take place that evening, his mood changes and he reveals a brutish side to his character. Throughout the performance, Goodman's Shylock veers from vulnerability and inner confusion (in the final moments he finds it almost impossible to carry out his revenge on Antonio) to seething hatred for those who have taught him to hate: 'The villainy you teach me, I will execute' (III.i.65). Without too much evidence upon which to base the claim, I feel that, in this Shylock, we have something nearer to the puritan voice we find in the pamphlets and essays of the sixteenth and seventeenth centuries, rather than a specifically Jewish voice. It is a point to think about.

The other major element in the production is Belmont, and in our first encounter with Portia and Nerissa (Act I, scene ii) we discover a melancholic mood not that far removed from the ethos of the nightclub in which we first encounter Antonio. The mood in Belmont is understandably fraught, and it is a tension that never really seems to leave, even in Act V. The Portia presented by Derbhle Crotty is as weighted down as Antonio – 'By my troth Nerissa, my little body is aweary of this great world' (I.ii.1–2) – and even in her clear passion for Bassanio we may detect a tension bred out of alienation. Portia has the capacity to 'shine like a good deed in a naughty world'; but she is bound by the will (imperative even in death through the substantive 'will') of her father. Here is a Portia that will always surprise us. The arrival of the Prince of Morocco is a pretext, in many productions, for a little covert racism, but here we find in both the presentation of Morocco himself, and in Portia's reaction to him, a recognition that anything could happen in this play. Morocco is a dashing and elegant figure, whose presence clearly unnerves Portia, and we gain the distinct feeling that she would like him to 'choose wisely'.

This passionate and tense Portia is not without sensitivity to Jessica's plight. Jessica, as we might expect in this production of characters seemingly on the edge of a nervous breakdown, is equally fragile. One of the most touching brief moments is when Jessica clings to Portia on introduction. While it is a brief moment, it carries more of a sense of humanity on the part of both women than we observe from all other characters in the performance.

The drama is played in this production between three complex and unpredictable figures: Antonio, Shylock and Portia. Intriguingly the viewer is left with no answers, but many questions.

5 Critical Assessments

Many groups of people lay claim to the ideological ownership of Shakespeare. Was he a Tory, a socialist, feminist, anti-Semitic, Roman Catholic, or, indeed, someone else altogether? The whole history concerning Shakespeare and his works has been a tale of ownership and/or rejection. It is a process that simultaneously sees him as transcendent of history and a man fashioned in the image of the time.

Shakespeare was a man of the late sixteenth and early seventeenth centuries to be taken account of: he was a player, poet, crafter of plays, and probable participant in some fairly suspect land enclosures. But even here the evidence is flimsy, and any simple critical interrogation will reveal that the meaning of documentary evidence is as open to textual readings as is any novel in contemporary critical discourse.

This critical assessment will take two broad lines of approach, of which the aim will be rather to alert the reader to the possibilities of criticism, than to prosecute one particular intellectual position. Criticism itself becomes the debate, with, in this case, *The Merchant of Venice* as its subject.

A chronological overview

Any chronological overview derived from selected historical observations will reveal Shakespeare's star rising and waning according to the moment. Finding a reliable starting point for critical responses to Shakespeare's work is by no means a simple task for, by 'critical response', we generally mean response to the literary text, without any particular reference to theatrical performance. However, our primary interest is in the theatrical event, but we must also recognize that direct access to performances is difficult. This means that critical analyses of performance tend to be restricted to the contemporary, where we have had direct experience of the production, or, at least, to productions in the relatively recent historical context, where we have access to documents appertaining to particular productions. In cases such as this, our reliance is on a well-constructed promptbook, and knowing how to read it. The recording of stage history, as may be seen in Chapter 3, is less a critical exercise than an anthology of impressions. Of course, there are elements of critical thought in such an exercise, but only elements. There are significant difficulties in establishing clear critical patterns for productions in Shakespeare's own lifetime. It is not until we reach the point of the publication of the First Folio in 1623 (seven years after Shakespeare's death) that we may glimpse responses to Shakespeare's work by his fellow-actors John Heminges and Henry Condell, as it were, through a glass darkly. The First Folio of 1623 was the first attempt to bring together Shakespeare's works in one volume, allotting to them Act divisions as well as those of the scenes. The First Folio also demonstrates the impetus towards a taxonomy of the plays by notional genre, e.g. tragedy, comedy, history, and romance.

Heminges and Condell had been leading members of the King's Men, following the death of Richard Burbage in 1619, and it was they who signed the epistle dedicatory and the address to the readers prefixed to the First Folio. (It is interesting to note in passing that the address is to the *readers*. Does this mark the point of the transition of Shakespeare's plays from the pre-literary theatrical event to the literary text?)

> Read him, therefore, and again and again, and if then you do not like him, surely you are in some manifest danger not to understand him . . . who, as he was a happy imitator of nature, was a most gentle expresser of it. His mind and hand went together, and what he thought he uttered with that easiness that we have scarce received from him a blot in his papers . . . for his wit can no more lie hid than it could be lost.

Ben Jonson added, under the title *To the memory of my beloved, The Author Master William Shakespeare AND what he hath left us*, his own poetic tribute of some 800 words. We may also find many comments on Shakespeare's work ranging from John Weever's sonnet *Ad Gulielmum Shakespeare* in *Epigrams* (1599) through to John Warren's sonnet *Of Master William Shakespeare* (1640) (Wells and Taylor, 1986, pp. xli–xlvii).

Despite the closure of the theatres in 1642, occasional performances did continue during the period of the Interregnum. Indeed, Cromwell licensed certain private entertainments, particularly school plays. While there was the continuance of limited and approved theatrical entertainments, there is no doubt that the Interregnum interrupted the development of native drama. The return of licensed theatres under the restoration of the monarchy (Charles II) produced an ambiguous mixture of attempts to revive that native drama of the public playhouses that operated between the 1570s and the 1630s (particularly the works of Fletcher and Jonson), and the introduction of continental (French and Spanish) dramaturgy.

The final four decades of the seventeenth century and the early decades of the eighteenth century saw an increasing influence of French neo-Classical rules in playwriting and literature, in both form and content. The tightly formal rules of such dramas with, in particular, the misapplication of aspects of the Aristotelian canon in the shape of the three unities (time, place, and action) meant that Shakespeare's complex structures of plot and sub-plot(s), shifting of place from country to country and disregard for a strict observation of time, were viewed as unstructured and somewhat undisciplined. A tenacious neo-Classical orthodoxy may be observed in the writings of, in particular, John Dryden and Thomas Rymer, who thought, according to Samuel Johnson, that Shakespeare's 'Romans were not sufficiently Roman'.

Moving on seven decades, François-Marie Voltaire, in *Appel à toutes les nations de l'Europe* (1761), 'censures his [Shakespeare's] kings as not completely royal'. While Voltaire attacked Shakespeare on the grounds that he offended against neo-Classical rules for literature, he simultaneously admired the humanity in Shakespeare's works, as did

Samuel Johnson, and was not above the occasional borrowing from Shakespeare (Johnson, 1968, pp. 59–113).

None of this meant an out-of-hand rejection of Shakespeare's plays. The aim of the 'new' theatre was, rather, to rescue Shakespeare from himself. In Nahum Tate's observation in 1680/81, when preparing his reworked version of Shakespeare's *King Lear*, he described Shakespeare's work as 'a heap of jewels, unstrung and unpolished, yet so dazzling in their disorder that I soon perceived I had seized a treasure'. Tate's adaptation of *King Lear*, which is probably best known for giving Lear and Cordelia a happy ending, sets out, as stated in Tate's dedication, to be a 'revival with alterations'.

Nicholas Rowe, in 1709, signalled unease with the perceived uneven mismatching in the structure of *The Merchant of Venice*:

> Tho' we have seen that Play Received and Acted as a Comedy, and the Part of the *Jew* perform'd by an Excellent Comedian, yet I cannot but think it was design'd Tragically by the Author. There appears in it such deadly Spirit of Revenge, such a savage Fierceness and fellness, and such a bloody designation of Cruelty and Mischief, as cannot agree either with the Style or Characters of Comedy.   (Wilders, 1969, p. 25)

Samuel Johnson's *Preface* (1765) to Shakespeare embodies the 'new' culture of a self-proclaimed 'age of reason'. Clearly there is a distance in cultural values, but by no means is there an outright dismissal; certainly not so on the part of Johnson. A part of the problem has to be in Johnson's view of Shakespeare more as a dramatic poet, as a poet of human nature, than as a playwright. The move away from the theatrical event, with all its inherent challenges to fixed values, that started with the production of the literary texts of the published quartos and folios, is now measured by a critical view that admits, above all, the pre-eminence of 'literature'. The value that Johnson finds in Shakespeare's work is, inevitably, conditioned by the neo-Classical principles espoused by the eighteenth century. Johnson's position here is, for the contemporary reader, somewhat double-edged. Whereas Johnson sees the 'condition of the age' (Shakespeare's, that is) as a state of ignorance, we may argue that an understanding of the social conditions of a cultural production produces an art form that, while it is different from the art form of a later age, is not necessarily inferior. At this point we may have touched on that aspect of eighteenth-century culture that assumed that humankind was inevitably progressing from one age to another.

> Every man's performances, to be rightly estimated, must be compared with the state of the age in which he lived, and with his own particular opportunities; and though to the reader a book be not worse or better for the circumstances of the authour, yet as there is always a silent reference of human works to human abilities, and as the enquiry, how far man may extend his designs, or how high he may rate his native force, is of far greater dignity than in what rank we shall place any particular performance, curiosity is always busy to discover the instruments, as well as to survey the workmanship, to know how much is to be ascribed to original powers, and how much to casual and adventitious help. (Johnson, 1968, p. 65)

There is an unevenness in *The Merchant of Venice* in the (mis)matching of seemingly disparate, but nevertheless – in this play - interdependent genres: the split between comedy/romance and tragedy; Portia not quite fitting into the accepted traditions of love interest; Bassanio falling somewhat short of the romantic hero; Shylock not quite fulfilling the function of tragedy (by whatever definition we choose); the sixteenth-century mercantile world of Venice mismatched with the pastoral Belmont seemingly left over from an earlier play. All these disparities were noted and censured in the eighteenth century, and Johnson finds himself both remonstrating with and seeming to defend Shakespeare.

> The censure which he has incurred by mixing comick and tragick scenes, as it extends to all his works, deserves more consideration. . . . Shakespeare's plays are not in the rigorous and critical sense either tragedies or comedies, but compositions of a distinct kind; exhibiting the real state of sublunary nature, which partakes of good and evil, joy and sorrow, mingled with endless variety of proportion and innumerable modes of combination; and expressing the course of the world, in which the loss of one is the gain of another; in which at the same time, the reveller is hasting to his wine, and the mourner burying his friend; in which the malignity of one is sometimes defeated by the frolick of

another; and many mischiefs and many benefits are done and hindered
without design.   (Johnson, 1968, p. 66)

At the heart of eighteenth-century cultural hegemony in England
were the concepts of rationality and enlightenment coupled with the
certainty of the inevitability of human progress. Rationality requires
rules, and even a sense of decorum, and this sense may help to understand the drive to bring order to Shakespeare's plays. His genius was
celebrated, but his works were flawed. The image of jewels badly
strung together, although expressed by Nahum Tate in the late seventeenth century, exemplifies the mingled disdain and admiration of
eighteenth-century taste.

The cultural reclamation of Shakespeare (and we may now dispense
with the distinction between the man and his works, for the man and
his works have become synonymous) gathered force in the last quarter
of the eighteenth century and the early decades of the nineteenth
century, though the theatrical foundations of bardolatry had already
been well laid by David Garrick. The critical reaction against the neo-
Classicist school of criticism prevalent in the eighteenth century was
expressed through what has come to be called the Romantic
Movement. The previous concern for plot structure, decorum and the
three unities gave way to a form of ideological individualism that was
primarily concerned with characterization. Characterization as the
main focus for critical reading, and indeed within the creative act itself,
was not, of course, new. We may argue that the seeds for a reification
of the individual as a distinct social element were sown with the evolution of the entrepreneurial mercantile society in the late sixteenth
century, as exemplified in the characters of Antonio (the merchant of
Venice) and Shylock (who we may term the 'banker' of Venice). What
we may discern in the early modern period, through to today, is a
concern for characterization over structure that demonstrates a
human being's interest in human beings.

If we are seeking critical signposts for this reaction against neo-
Classicism we may cite John Locke's *Essay Concerning Human
Understanding*, written *circa* 1687 but not published until 1690. Further
into the eighteenth century Edmund Burke should be noted in his
Enquiry into the Origin of Our Ideas of the Sublime and the Beautiful (1757).

Further on, and more central to the Romantic Movement, we should also note Percy Bysshe Shelley's *Defence of Poetry* (1821), and, as possibly the foremost Romantic critic, William Hazlitt's critical writing on *The Merchant of Venice*.

As was clear in the chapter on the play's stage history, much of the descriptive and critical evidence from this period tends to focus on the character of Shylock. Unlike very early treatments of Shylock where the emphasis tended towards treating him as either a comic Pantalone figure, or as a villain, the Romantic critic favoured the construction of Shylock as a sufferer for his race, and as much sinned against as sinning; a character of tragic potential. As critical accounts and theatrical productions in our contemporary world demonstrate, this approach is still a favoured method by which our post-Holocaust society attempts to resolve the tension between the revered work of Shakespeare and the unease with which we encounter sixteenth-century attitudes towards Jewish people.

Modern critical readings

The remainder of this chapter will be structured under a series of sub-headings each of which represents a particular critical approach to Shakespeare. It will not attempt to be all-inclusive, but merely to give the reader a sense of the ideological map in modern times. Nor will there be any attempt to espouse any one particular approach, the aim being simply to represent as objectively as possible the main tenets of each critical approach to Shakespeare's work. The reader will, inevitably, find that different critical positions appear, occasionally, to occupy similar territory. This is to be expected when we understand that no one way of thinking is entirely separated from another, and that we are all part of a cultural continuum. There are, however, moments in cultural history where claims are made for the absolute truth; this is often referred to as essentialism and, often, declares its independence (transcendence?) from other forms. However, experience does seem to suggest we cannot separate one way of thinking from another. That one way of thinking often contains the intellectual seeds of what will follow, even though the succeeding ideological formation denies the preceding one; in the end we cannot divorce Marx from his debt to Hegel regarding dialectical philosophy, although the latter's conclusions embraced spiritual essentialism while Marx's conclusions led to materialist dialectics.

Humanist readings of Shakespeare

Any consideration of cultural criticism must perforce include humanist readings. However, the term has a variety of contemporary meanings and they may often appear to contradict each other. Of course 'humanism' may simply refer to the state of being human, or in a very contemporary sense, humanitarianism, which means caring for the well being of other human beings. Furthermore, as institutional religion in the West commands fewer and fewer adherents, there is an increasing demand for secular humanist rites of passage to replace religious funerals, and so, in this sense, humanism seeks to construct secular moral codes. These secular moral codes may well draw on the Judeo-Christian European traditions, but eschew the spiritual dimension. More specifically, the English dramatic Renaissance, of which Shakespeare is a central figure, is often referred to as the rebirth of Classical humanist values (or we may say 'aesthetics'). This does not mean that English society of the sixteenth and seventeenth centuries was a secular society, far from it. In this specific case, humanism needs to be viewed against the background of medieval society. A useful example may be seen in the distinction, on a European level, between late medieval Italian paintings of the Madonna and Child and the early Italian Renaissance depictions of that subject. The Madonna and Child painted by Cimabue in the period before the Italian Renaissance shows an idealized mother with child that represents the subject at an iconic level – the Virgin and the Christ Child. On the other hand, Giotto's early Italian Renaissance Madonna and Child, apart from his treatment of perspective, depicts a real Tuscan peasant woman holding a child of flesh and blood towards which we have the opportunity to develop a 'human' response. The 'human being' becomes the subject for art, rather than an iconic figure that denies the humanity of flesh. In much the same way, we may see the individualistic human-centred characterization of Elizabethan and Jacobean playwriting as a distinct move away from earlier medieval dramas where people are represented by personified human qualities such as Truth, Beauty, or Good Deeds. By way of example we may also observe how Christopher Marlowe, in *Dr Faustus*, deliberately employs the old technique of personified human qualities such as the Good Angel, Bad Angel, and even the Old Man, who is in effect 'Goodness', Morality, in contrast to the very humanist portrayal of John Faustus. The outcome is that Renaissance Humanism did not necessarily mean a rejection of religion (although atheism was fashionable among certain of the literati such as Marlowe, it was necessarily a view held in private); it was more that the human being was the focus of attention, even in religion.

Belief in human reason and creativity are the liberating factors in a humanistic ideology, and, when we encounter Shakespeare, we see humanism embodied in the word: dramatic, rhetorical and poetic. It is difficult, if not impossible, to quantify why human beings should respond to each other's needs but we may take it that this is what is implicit in human nature: a subjective response that 'springs from sharing the same material life' (Eagleton, 1986, p. 44). Such observations in relationship to our understanding of a humanistic approach may be seen to be embedded in Shylock's speech, when he refuses to provide a rationale for his seeming inhuman behaviour.

> (Master of passion) sways it to the mood
> Of what it likes or loathes, – now for your answer:
> As there is no firm reason to be rend'red
> Why he cannot abide a gaping pig,
> Why he a harmless necessary cat,
> Why he a woollen bagpipe, but of force
> Must yield to such inevitable shame,
> As to offend himself being offended:
> So I can give no reason, nor I will not,
> More than a lodg'd hate, and a certain loathing
> I bear Antonio, that I follow thus
> A losing suit against him! – are you answered?
>
> (IV.i.51–62)

Shylock refuses Portia's money, and insists on the spirit of the law being recognized. Portia, however, pursues the logic of the law's letter. Shylock's adherence to the spirit of the law can be interpreted as his belief that human flesh cannot be quantified. This is unusual for this society where human beings do seem to be accounted in terms of their commodity value, as we see quite clearly in the terms of Portia's father's will, in which she is embodied in the substance of the caskets. Does this mean that Shylock emerges from the trial as the moral superior to Portia? The intrinsic quality of human relationships, good or ill, appears to transcend mere monetary value, and this observation may lead us to consider, then, the relationship between these 'human relationships' in juxtaposition to the mercantile systems that both allow, and condemn, Shylock and his fellow Jews in Venice.

Psychoanalytical critical readings and Shakespeare

It is difficult to avoid the assumption that humanist and psychoanalytical readings share many similar concerns, focusing as they do on human character; or more precisely in the case of psychoanalytical theory, on the human psyche. We may, however, be allowed the distinction that, whereas a humanist reading focuses on the actions of the fictional character, a psychoanalytical approach is concerned with the ways by which the psyches of human beings are formed – fictional or real. Indeed psychoanalytical work in the field of drama has produced an interesting cross-fertilization between the commentary on fictional characters and the way an involvement in playing the fictional character is, in the field of 'psychodrama', a means to resolve human dysfunction. As an aside, it is interesting to note that a result of the 'universalizing' of Shakespeare's works as the template for human conditions has produced, in the practice of psychodrama, the use of Shakespeare's plays as the means to efficacy.

The two names in psychoanalytic theory that are central to critical readings of the theatre are Sigmund Freud and Jacques Lacan. The initial work of Freud forms the basis of theories of understanding of the psyche, and Lacan's development of Freud into theories of language in relation to the psyche relates this area of study to dramatic works. There are many other developments in the field of psychoanalytical theory, but most of these relate to specific ideological positions. In particular, note should be taken of the work of Julia Kristeva in feminist theory and its contribution to psychoanalytical approaches (Laplanche and Pontalis, 1973).

Freud's basic premise argued that human beings are 'made' rather than 'born'. This premise, of course, challenges certain aspects of humanist thought. At a simple level, we may understand Freud's theories as proposing a constructed but fragmented human psyche that is gendered, but not necessarily gendered in the way that contemporary feminist cultural theoreticians would argue. Freud's emphasis on the slotting of individuals into various sexual and familial roles has been challenged by later theories. Essentially Freud's work suggests hidden truths in our language that we may not be aware of at the time of utterance. Immediately we may see how an approach such as this will lead to questions about the underlying state of Shylock's mind, or feelings that Portia may not be aware she possesses regarding her dead father.

Freud certainly has some interesting observations on *The Merchant of Venice* and, in particular, the matter of the three suitors choosing Portia's caskets. Freud's view is that Bassanio, as the third suitor, has the most difficult task in that 'glorification of lead as against gold and silver is but little and has a forced ring about it. If in psycho-analytical practice we were confronted with such a speech, we should suspect concealed motives behind the unsatisfying argument' (Freud, 1913, p. 59 and ref. Bassanio, III.ii.73–114). Freud posits the argument that the choice of the three caskets has its origins in a variety of ancient myths, particularly those that deal with a man being asked to choose between three women; Paris choosing between the three goddesses, Hera, Aphrodite and Athena, being the most obvious example. Freud pursues his argument:

> If we had to do with a dream, it would at once occur to us that the caskets are also women, symbols of the essential thing in woman, and therefore of a woman herself. . . . If we let ourselves assume the same substitution in the story, then the casket scene in *The Merchant of Venice* really becomes

the inversion we suspected. With one wave of the hand, such as usually happens only in fairy-tales . . . we see that the subject is an idea from human life, a man's choice between three women. (Freud, 1913, p. 60)

Bassanio, in choosing lead, refers to its 'paleness', which 'moves me more than eloquence' (III.ii.106). (While there is some question over whether the word should be plainness or paleness, the latter is generally an editor's preferred option, as it is in our text.) Freud pursues this option seeing paleness – its striking pallor – as a symbol of death. How this image may relate to the romantic narrative in *The Merchant of Venice* is not immediately clear, unless a link may be made with the world of Belmont coming to Venice because of the threat of death to Antonio. However, Freud offers the imagery of contradiction in dreams as a possible answer.

> However, contradictions of a certain kind, replacements by the exact opposite, offer no serious difficulty to analytic interpretation. We shall not this time take our stand on the fact that contraries are constantly represented by one and the same element in the modes of expression used by the unconscious, such as dreams. But we shall remember that there are forces in mental life tending to bring about replacement in the opposite, such as the so-called replacement by the opposite, and it is just in the discovery of such hidden forces that we look for the reward of our labours.   (Freud, 1913, p. 66)

Bassanio hopes to overcome death, or at least the consequence of failure, by choosing the third casket. As Paris chose the third goddess, Aphrodite – who, in her earlier forms, had associations with Hades before relinquishing that role to Persephone – so Bassanio chooses lead with its death pallor in the hope of the opposite outcome.

Jacques Lacan further developed Freud's theories, but stressed the importance of language for the human psyche (or as we now prefer, consciousness and unconsciousness). The argument finds points of contact with many different and often conflicting ideologies emerging in the late nineteenth and early twentieth centuries, as with the relationship between consciousness and language in Marxism. Lacan defines the human psyche (or consciousness) as a linguistic entity. At a simple level, without language, we do not exist. Furthermore, Lacan argues that we (the linguistic entity) engage with ourselves and the world at two levels: the imaginary and the symbolic. The imaginary is associated with states of dysfunction and psychosis (does this mean that all art is some kind of arrested condition?). The symbolic engages in a flexible discourse where change is always possible, and thus promotes acceptable social relationships. Both of these levels of register create as many questions and answers as each other when we focus on theatrical events and may form questions for discussion in the chapter on *The Merchant of Venice* in performance.

The various forms of psychoanalytical approach allow two ways of relating to drama and theatre. First of all there is the temptation to analyse the state of mind of the author, as when we attempt to divine the author's intention in creating the work of art. Freud would certainly place the work of art as a slip of the psyche (or as we often say colloquially, a Freudian slip) revealing the author's state of mind. Or we may engage in an exercise to psychoanalyse the characters in order to draw out meanings that are not immediately apparent in their actions. The conventions of acting devised by Constantin Stanislavski would appear to have much in common, at an intuitive rather than strictly scientific level, with psychoanalytical approaches to both the creation and critical analysis of theatre. While Stanislavski's approach to acting is widely accepted in its most simple form in the western theatre, there is a tendency towards essentialism in its acceptance that needs to be balanced by other conventions. This is particularly apposite in the case of Shakespeare's plays, where the poetic form of language shapes both character and action. Thus, we may ask if those, essentially, late nineteenth-century approaches to theatre making are entirely appropriate, in their determination to present an illusion that suggests 'that this is really happening', when the dramatic form and theatrical provenance of Shakespeare's works are grounded in an overtly poetic form. Our questions arise from the experience that Shakespeare offers, not only the poetry of drama, but also the poetry of theatre.

Feminist critical readings and Shakespeare

It is interesting to note that, even in a patriarchal society (a society in which authority and power are invested in the male, particularly in the father of a family), Shakespeare's plays present us with a surprisingly complex picture of women's roles. It is largely due to the development of feminist critical readings in the twentieth century (and continuing in the twenty-first century) that the dilemmas of these female characters and issues of gender are brought into the light of our critical discourse. We should also note that in the original context of making the theatrical event, the women's parts were written in the knowledge that they must be played by men. Far from this necessarily meaning that the female characters were reduced to accommodate the limitations of male mimicry, we find that certain plays set questions regarding the nature of the performance of gender; we may cite the example of *As You Like It*, where the ambiguity of gender forced on Rosalind by Duke Frederick also creates by default the gender games that abound between Rosalind and Orlando.

Feminist criticism alerts us to the relationships between women and men, and how we may see the world in ways that challenge patriarchal hegemony. Furthermore, it enables us to understand how women and men in their gender identities are constructed as social creatures. So, for example, gender is understood as a social construct as distinct from sexual identity. While gender and sex are linked, the distinction between sexes is largely determined by the presence of ovaries or testicles in the body. Gender is more a matter of femininity or masculinity, and those concepts may be better understood as cultural than as biological constructs. 'But biology alone cannot explain the elaborate and varied systems cultures have employed in distinguishing masculine and feminine domains and qualities. In some times and places women have been associated with the body and men with reason; but the reverse is also true' (Wells and Orlin, 2003, p. 411).

Shakespeare (the body of work) has, as with many other critical approaches, formed the focus for a formidable corpus of feminist criticism since the 1970s. We should understand that this should not be seen as an affirmation of the established (male) canon, but more as a critique of that (male-dominated) hegemony. Initially, feminist criticism focused on the female characters whose role in performance challenges normative female roles, and, inevitably, elements of this approach were psychoanalytical in their methods. However, the 1980s saw the development of a feminist criticism that sought to historicize the role of women in Shakespeare – as opposed to the notion of timeless and universal models of female behaviour – within the re-making of each period of history. Feminist critical readings of the original period of theatrical production have challenged the concept in which the female is passionate and less rational, and an imperfect version of the perfect male model presented by male players playing women. In the comedies, such as *Twelfth Night* and *As You like It*, the boy players are allowed to be seen as boys through the necessity of the female character having to adopt male disguise in order to be able to function in certain social conditions. However, the problem becomes more complex – and threatening – when, as Jean E. Howard points out, 'the mannish woman and the womanish man are more problematic and threatening', as in the instances of Volumnia in *Coriolanus*, the unmanly Henry VI, or, indeed, Lady Macbeth (Wells and Orlin, 2003, p. 420).

How may these ideas help us in our understanding of *The Merchant of Venice*? The early line, 'In Belmont is a lady richly left,' gives us the main narrative drive to gain a highly marriageable woman for Bassanio. (Interestingly, the venture does seem to require a male team effort, even to the extent of drawing Shylock into the endeavour.) However, a certain level of feminist reading (remembering that there are many different forms of feminist ideology) might draw together aspects of class together with gender status. Many of the sixteenth-century merchants, once they had made their money through trade, sought to legitimize their social position by moving into the landed classes where 'real' status still lay. We may cite, in this instance, Bassanio's hoped-for move from the Rialto to Belmont. Furthermore, while we may perceive Portia initially as the marriage object, trapped and commodified by her father's will, another Portia is emerging before Bassanio even reaches Belmont. The Portia of a feminist reading of the play, if we may be allowed a theatrical metaphor, stage-manages everything from the casket scene with Bassanio, through to the Trial and finishing with the final flourish in her trick with the rings.

Bruce R. Smith proposes the notion that, 'In the [*possible*] love triangle of Antonio–Bassanio–Portia, the middle position is occupied, not by a woman, but by a young man, just as it is in Shakespeare's sonnets. Bassanio figures as an erotic object for both Antonio and Portia' (Smith, 2003, p. 447). In other words, there is the potential for an interpretation that reverses the traditional male and female roles of Portia and Bassanio. The point is not that Shakespeare wrote a feminist play, he didn't, but that a multiplicity of meanings may be drawn from the text, the legitimacy of which depends on close reading of the extant work.

One further point that may result from a feminist reading of the play is to note that, unlike some other of Shakespeare's female characters, Portia chooses disguise in order that she may rescue a male character. Whereas Viola and indeed Rosalind are forced to adopt male persona for self-protection in a dangerous male world, Portia's disguise is to do with the need for empowerment. We recognize that a patriarchal society would not allow her the freedom to demonstrate her skill with the law; nevertheless she is the one character who seems to be in command of the situation. However, while subverting earlier expectations, Portia does not become the 'mannish woman' in the shape of Volumnia or Lady Macbeth and become a subsequent problematic or disruptive element in the male society of the play. We should finish with a question, rather than an answer. Does the fact that Portia commands nearly every scene in which she appears (we may even argue that she exercises a degree of control in the scenes with Morocco and Arragon) while avoiding the failures of the problematic 'mannish woman' have more to do with the play being a comedy, than it does with Portia representing some kind of new woman? (After all, Volumnia and Lady Macbeth were later creations.)

Feminist criticism has brought gender studies into the performance of Shakespeare, and has raised, and brought into a shared discourse, the added layers of class, race, sexuality, and indeed questions relating to masculinity. This matter will be taken further under the sub-heading of 'cultural materialism'.

Postcolonial critical readings of Shakespeare

The end of the Second World War effectively marked the end, or at least the beginning of the end, of the Western European colonization of large parts of the world in the quest for empire. The break-up of the European empires has brought about many effects, among them being the loss of role and clear political identity on the world stage, and the need to adjust to evolving as multi-racial societies (some with more success than others). Postcolonial critical readings focus on the effects of Western European imperialism on the rest of the world after 400 years of colonization and political and social domination. The concept is concerned with the past, but the prefix 'post' also implies a concern with the simultaneous effects of liberation and continuing oppression by more indirect means. We readily under-stand how multinational corporations may be continuing western domination – and exploitation – of the global market place; less easily do we understand the continuing unequal cultural relationship between western cultures and those cultures they once controlled. In particular, postcolonial critical readings help us to understand how art and literature are still inextricably bound up with 'colonial' economies. As Edward Said points out in his 'Introduction' to *Culture and Imperialism*, 'Most professional humanists . . . are unable to make the connection between the prolonged and sordid cruelty of such practices as slavery, colonialist and racial oppression, and imperial subjection on the one hand, and the poetry, fiction, and philosophy of the society that engages in these practices on the other' (Said, 1994, p. xiv).

A postcolonial reading of Shakespeare offers two aids to under-standing the works: first, there is an approach to how early modern English society defined and related to non-European (and non-Christian) races; secondly, it aids a focus on how Shakespeare is received in non-western cultures and, in particular, those cultures that were once subjugated within the British (English?) Empire. In the latter case, we may further observe how, in many instances, the colo-nization by 'Shakespearean culture' has also, in its turn, afforded the colonized the opportunity to re-make Shakespeare and appropriate the works to their own cultural conditions. By way of an aside, we do need to be aware of how Shakespearean currency works in unexpected, and often unwanted, ways. It is by no means unusual for an overseas research student who is studying Shakespeare's theatre at a British university to insist that it is 'English Shakespeare' that they work on, and not some 'inferior' adaptation. Sometimes the imperative comes from the student's own desire to 'join the hierarchical club'; sometimes the insistence is driven by the student's government which, often as not, is paying the fees.

Postcolonial readings when combined with feminist critical readings afford further possibilities of breaking through monolithic ideas of racial and gender types. We may further posit the notion that humanist readings with their emphasis on individuality may be 'radicalized' in the light of the interplay between these developing discourses.

In respect of *The Merchant of Venice*, we may think back to Antony Sher's approach to playing Shylock. At one level, the 'orientalizing' of Shylock as a Turkish Jew may appear to fall into the trap of marginalizing him as simply 'other' and therefore exotic, thus confirming in the Venetian Christian view his dangerousness and untrustworthiness in that society. However, leaving this as a literary critical view would be to discount the stage actions employed by Sher as Shylock and Bill Alexander as director. The sheer force and continuing verbal and gestural violence shown towards Shylock in this production subvert a simple sense that Shylock is merely exotic, and bring to the foreground the racism of the Christian Venetians. Furthermore, the fascinating moment of Sher's onstage demonstration against the South African (Nationalist) ambassadorial representative serves as an excellent example of postcolonial collision embedded in stage action: a Jewish South African gay actor playing an 'oriental' Jew, confronting the South African Nationalist politician with a black member of the cast of *The Merchant of Venice*.

A postcolonial reading of *The Merchant of Venice* is not restricted to concerns over the stage representation of Shylock the Jew. In one sense, we may argue that issues to do with colonialism and imperialism are embedded in the play's title. By and large, mercantile trade drove the growth and expansion of the British Empire and much of the dramatic tension of this play has its origins in the vagaries and uncertainties of trade abroad. Bassanio's need for capital in order to embark on his venture to win the highly marriageable Portia would have been provided, in normal circumstances, by the wealth derived from Antonio's overseas trading ventures. However, because Antonio's ships are all at sea (both literally and later, they believe, metaphorically) the recourse to Shylock's money-lending is needed. In this way the dramatic tensions are born out of the interrelation of 'romance' and mercantile adventure.

Postcolonial theory cannot be tied down to a monolithic perspective, given the sheer complexity and ambiguity of all the varied cultures that have been subjugated through the imperialist drives of the past 400 years. Nor can any notion of postcolonial reading be restricted to the past, as cultural colonialism, in its many forms, is still a driving force.

Materialist critical readings and Shakespeare

In the two previous critical approaches the text, whether that be in its literary or its performative form, tends to be treated in isolation from the material conditions that produced it. A broadly materialist approach embeds the 'text' in the material, social, and historical conditions that produced it or continue to produce it. The relationship between 'text' and moment of production differs according to which particular historical and/or cultural context is the focus of our critical reading. Raymond Williams theorized culture as a site of struggle divided into dominant (or hegemonic), residual and emergent formations (Williams, 1980). Shakespeare and his works function as a site of cultural struggle that, rather than confirming Shakespeare as a conservative icon, reveals the potential contradictions in social relations. It would seem as if Shakespeare has as much to say to the materialist, as the materialist has to say about Shakespeare (Jameson, 1981).

A 'conservative' Marxist reading of *The Merchant of Venice* might observe the meeting between the competing mercantile worlds of a scheming Bassanio and the agrarian feudal world of Portia creating a class tension in the play. But, if the production presents the play as a simple reflection of those worlds, which are brought together through marriage, the internal contradictions of the worlds and the characters remain unexposed.

Cultural materialism

A classic Marxist approach to Shakespearean criticism may well allow us to expose the socio-economic contexts of *The Merchant of Venice*, just as a humanist approach will focus on human relationships and a psychoanalytical approach will afford us the means to wonder at the psychological motives that drive both author and characters. However, all of these critical readings, taken in isolation, may be seen as presenting us with only a partial picture, wherein the play simply reflects certain aspects of human social life. Such single-minded readings take no account of how these elements might inform each other, or how a performance of the play not only reflects social values, but is actively a producer, as well as a product, of our cultures. Moreover, Raymond Williams initiated 'the convention of inserting the critic/writer into his/her own discourse as a physical presence, a character in the action. . . . The device is an act of critical self-consciousness, impossibly representing the author as a speaker who is both producer of, and a subject within, his own writing' (Holderness, 2003, p. 250). Not so much a case of art imitating (reflecting) life, but the human subject creating life.

Two critical schools, one in the United States of America, the other British, that have arisen in the latter half of the twentieth century are known as 'new historicism' (USA) and 'cultural materialism' (Britain). While the two critical readings have much in common in that they both observe that it is unproductive to separate various ideological approaches such as Marxism, feminism, psychoanalytical approaches, and postcolonialism and so on, arguing that they are all significant elements of the critical discourse, new historicism and cultural materialism do eventually differ, in part because they have evolved from different cultures. For our purposes, we will consider only cultural materialism (Greenblatt, 1988).

Materialism, as we may now understand it, should not be

misconstrued in the colloquial use of the term as meaning an over-concern with the acquisition of material wealth or goods. 'Materialism', in its philosophical sense, is opposed to idealism. The insistence is that culture cannot transcend the material conditions of its creation. That means that it challenges the notion that Shakespeare's genius is so great that his works have universal meaning transcendent of historical conditions; any play by Shakespeare is therefore understood to be related to the contexts of its production (theatrical or literary), not as a reflection of that historical moment, but as a part of the institutions of that time.

'Culture' in this context is to be understood in its analytical sense, as employed in the social sciences and anthropology, rather than its 'evaluative' sense, when it carries a suggestion of value judgement (high culture versus popular culture, e.g. 'Mozart is more important than Hip Hop'). To use culture in this analytic sense is to seek to describe 'the whole system of significations by which a society or a section of it understands itself and its relations with the world' (Dollimore and Sinfield, 1985, p. vii). In this sense 'high culture' is just one of a system of significations, by which our interest in culture may allow our attention to be drawn to an adaptation of Shakespeare (*Kiss Me Kate*) just as much as to the extant texts of *The Taming of the Shrew*. Nor should we forget that Shakespeare embraced many forms of theatrical entertainment; the writer who made *Love's Labours Lost* was also responsible for *Hamlet*.

The formulation of cultural materialist criticism, certainly since the 1980s, has often taken place through readings of Shakespeare. Admittedly the leading practitioners have come from the ranks of literary criticism (Alan Sinfield, Jonathan Dollimore, John Drakakis, Graham Holderness and others), but all articulate a keen understanding of the theatre as a site of ideological struggle. This point is easily understood when we read of the range (and often rage) of reception given to the production of the plays throughout their history. Cultural materialism seeks to bring us to recognize and understand the synergy to be gained in an exchange of discourses between the dissident or subversive voices in the complexities of feminist, post-colonial and class readings.

One approach to *The Merchant of Venice* offered by a cultural materialist critical reading is to understand how the world of the play, that is the fictional Venice of the play, objectifies the human body by divorcing it from any sense of humanity. It is doubtful whether we could argue the case for any one character being valued wholly for his or her humanity. There is sufficient evidence to point to Portia's commodity value in terms of her wealth being a primary motivation in Bassanio's mind. Whatever the relationship between Antonio and Bassanio has been, Antonio, once Bassanio has Portia in his sights, has a value in the capital he can provide for the young entrepreneur's venture to Belmont. It is obvious that no one in the Christian society of Venice would think of approaching Shylock if it were not for the fact that he possesses a commodity value in ready cash. Even Jessica may be seen in terms of her stolen 'dowry'. However, it is ironic that the bond that Shylock demands is not in the form of cash interest or even property, but in the shape of Antonio himself, or at least a portion of him. A perverse circle has been turned. The use value of objects has been supplanted by their monetary value. The value of people for their humanity has been dislocated by their immediate value as financial assets. But now the human body has become the ultimate commodity. Even money is now secondary to this object, as we see when Shylock considers taking only three times the amount he loaned to Antonio when it is clear that the latter has lost his case in court. But what value does a pound of Antonio's flesh possess? Obviously none on the open market, unless people are turning to cannibalism. The only value is in the strength of Shylock's desire for revenge. The human body, so far removed from humanity in this play, has now achieved the power to fuel and satiate human emotions; it has become reunited with 'humanity', but in a most grotesque version created by inhumane social conditions.

In conclusion to this section we may take note of Marx's argument in his *Theses on Feurbach*, that the point is not merely to interpret the world, but to change it. All good theatre, I would argue, of whatever ideological persuasion, seeks to understand how theatre may affect the world and the people who inhabit it.

6 Commentary

This chapter, which is the main focus of the book, is placed last, as the primary function of the preceding chapters has been to provide the necessary foundation upon which we may now consider the play in performance. Given the cultural pre-eminence accorded to Shakespeare's works, it is impossible to approach any of the plays without a pre-formed idea, drawn from a variety of sources, of how the play should be performed. Our task is to consider the meanings that have been created through the play's reception as a whole, the dramatic structure formed by all the scenes, and each scene in turn, with the aim of raising questions regarding the ways in which the play may be performed.

Having, in the preceding chapters, raised a number of questions concerning the cultural and intellectual context, key performances and screen versions, and critical assessment, we are now equipped to consider the challenges raised by performance, not in some vague cultural vacuum, but with a clear sense of how the very practical materiality of theatrical production is intrinsically a part of cultural production and sensibility. The questions are those that face contemporary actors, stage managers, directors, and scenic and costume designers, in the rehearsal room and on the stage. Our interrogation of the play's performative potential will take the form of a 'virtual' workshop with actors and directors. However, this is not meant to be a taxonomy of the 'do's' and 'don'ts' for theatre makers. The purpose of the workshop approach is to engage the reader, who may well not be a theatre maker, or have any intention of being so, in an understanding of the questions that must be addressed if we are to understand the play as it becomes alive on the stage.

Our purpose is not further to record productions that have

engaged our interest, or for me as author to visualize some ideal performance that would satisfy my aims and aspirations. The hope is that we will be able to evolve a performance vocabulary, derived from the text and from knowledge of the material business of making theatre, in order that we are able to develop an imaginative theatrical engagement with the action, persons and argument of *The Merchant of Venice* in John Russell Brown's edition (1967). The prime purpose of the commentary is to envisage an exploratory workshop, rather than a production.

The theatre maker's initial questions

In this section we are going to address the range of interpretative questions any theatre practitioner must tackle as a preface to the rehearsals. Here we must take account of the play's general themes and cultures and how they feature in the rhythms of the dramatic narrative, and how we may 'read' them today; and moreover, if we are to have an interval in our production, what effect the placing of an interval might have on the narrative. At the centre of all these considerations are the actors who will give life to the characters and the dramatic narrative. What role may the actors play in the whole process? How do the actors relate to a director? Or perhaps we should reverse the question and ask how the director should relate to her or his actors? And underlying all these considerations is the question of the performance space in which the play will be given life. What implications are there for the play's meaning if the performance is to be staged on an 'open', or on an 'enclosed' stage? Does the difference between shapes of performance space demand different kinds of relationship between the actor and the audience?

What follows now is a series of loosely held together thoughts that form the kind of creative questions that theatre makers, from writers to actors and directors through to stage managers, need to pose about the creative process. They certainly should not be read as formally constructed critical interrogations, which, while they necessarily inform the creative process, would constrain creativity if allowed to drive the process. The questions raised will focus on the issues we will need to address, and to give theatrical life to, in the scene-by-scene workshop that is to follow in the next section. There is an important note to be made at this point with respect to the play's structure. The scene, rather than the Act, is the important unit in the narrative structure of Shakespeare's play. There are twenty scenes in *The Merchant of Venice* with twelve being set in Venice and eight in Belmont. However, while the interplay between scenes will be of most use to us, for ease of cross-reference to our chosen text the Act and the scene number in that Act will be used.

Venice and Belmont

The two worlds are different in more ways than geographical and physical distance would seem to suggest. They represent two very different social orders, with Venice presented as a harsh, proto-capitalist mercantile world embodied in the Shylock plot, and Belmont as a rural feudal retreat embodying the romance plots of Portia and Bassanio, Jessica and Lorenzo, and, to a lesser extent, Nerissa and Gratiano. Much traditional criticism and twentieth-century performance has attempted to contrive a reconciliation between the two worlds that Shakespeare has set apart.

- Is this apparent dissimilarity a dramatic flaw in the play?
- Or is there a more interesting dramatic tension in the juxta-position of the two worlds?
- Or, is it a possibility that there are more likenesses than differ-ences between these two worlds?
- Are these worlds so decidedly distinct from each other, since it is clear that Portia is able to move with confidence between them?

While the lives of the inhabitants of Venice are bound in contracts, bonds, and the overriding scheme of the legal system, the ultimate tension in performance has to be in the irony that Shylock rejects money for the spirit of his bond.

- In doing so, is he not behaving in a more human way than the Christians?
- Might we argue that Shylock is acting upon the *spirit of the bond*, whereas Portia's ultimate 'winning' of the legal case is through a pedantic reading of the *letter of the law*?
- Does Portia, after her eloquent plea for the spirit of mercy, not simply win by a cheap trick and so leave Shylock as the moral victor?

This raises the whole issue of how we read texts. A close (literary) critical reading has to be accurate and true to what is on the page of the text, whereas a performance has to embody meaning beyond the text through intonation, gesture and action. Portia reads the text/bond and states that no blood may be spilt. Shylock takes the fuller meaning of the text/bond to imply that of course blood may be spilt. Portia's reading is pedantic. Shylock's action may be awful in its motive and consequence, but his is a very human passion.

Portia is good at behaving in a Venetian manner, whereas the Christians, Antonio, Bassanio and Gratiano, seem to be floundering, incapable of mustering a rational argument.

- Is it the case that when one person enters the world of another a kind of topsy-turvydom takes place, and if so, what implication does this have for the acting range we may need to employ in order to communicate these changes of level?

While in Belmont, Portia is a creature in thrall to 'romance' of a particularly sixteenth-century kind in that her future is subject to the caskets of gold, silver and lead, to say nothing of the legal text of her father's will. So, our initial questions must focus on the nature of Belmont and Portia, while she inhabits that place, for Belmont cannot simply be relegated to being a second player to Venice. If we are to relegate Belmont in this fashion, we must accept that Shakespeare made a mistake, and that the play should end with the trial scene and Shylock's demise.

The late sixteenth century was a period in our history that saw the gradual emergence of a mercantile society in London and a social and economic class that we may describe as the precursor of the financial and manufacturing middle classes that developed out of the industrial revolution. The England of *The Merchant of Venice* had a Venice in London, and the many Belmonts in the shires were aware of the gradual shift in economic and political power from the rural agrarian to the mercantile.

'Belmont', with a dark underbelly hidden beneath its pastoral surface, exists in many of Shakespeare's comedies. In some instances it is in contrast to a harsher world, as Arden is to the Court of Duke Frederick in *As You Like It*. In other examples the pastoral world, or retreat, is not in contrast to another place, but signifies a place divided against itself. Don John is a malign calculating presence in the superficially benign Sicily of *Much Ado About Nothing*, and the fates of Antonio and Malvolio expose a fundamental unease in the lotus-eating Illyria of *Twelfth Night*.

- But what does Belmont mean?

The literal meaning of Belmont is 'beautiful hill'. Bassanio, in his speech describing Portia to Antonio (scene i, lines 161–75), likens Portia to the Golden Fleece, which was the object of Jason's quest in ancient Greek mythology. While many Renaissance scholars interpreted Jason's quest as one after wisdom, Bassanio's quest, which after all does contain an element of fortune-hunting, serves to elide Portia and Belmont; we may take the image further to suggest that the beautiful hill, set above the plain of Venice, is Portia's *mons veneris*. Belmont is Portia.

One further point to note is the association of Belmont/Portia with music. Music is played while Bassanio makes his choice of the caskets and that has its own significance in performance and meaning – and music underlies Lorenzo and Jessica's scene together (Act V, particularly lines 54–65) at the end of the play. This is something to be taken into account in a staging of the play.

- Lorenzo refers to the music of the spheres as they turn in their celestial orbits, which takes music to a metaphysical and elemental level: the music of Heaven. How does this affect our interpretation of Belmont at this point in the play?

- Music, at this level of interpretation, signals a reconciliation of hitherto dispersed souls, which we may read as integral to a comedic ending. But how does this relate to the past disturbances and to disruptions still to come in the form of the trick with the rings and the unresolved ambiguity of Jessica's position?

- How, then, does Belmont relate to Venice and conventional understandings of comedy?

- Does the 'music' of Belmont relate to a yearning for a lost pastoral world that is understood in almost metaphysical terms?

- If Belmont is Portia, how do we portray her 'descent' into Venice? (We may need to return to this question when we think about Portia's male disguise.)

Shylock and his position as a Jew, and anti-Semitism and how we address it in performance

Legally speaking, there could be no Jews living in London in the late sixteenth century. They were banished from England by Edward I in 1290 and not formally re-admitted until 1655, by Oliver Cromwell. As an aside, we may wish to remember the seemingly sympathetic tone in Puritan references to Jews in tracts of the time. Puritans and Jews were both marginalized groups until the Puritan ascendancy with Oliver Cromwell. Moreover, we may note, when we come to analyse the scenes in Shylock's house, a marked similarity to Puritanism, particularly in an overriding sense of austerity. Indeed, popular culture of the time attributed usury to Puritans, as the emergent merchant class, as much as it did to Jews. The question regarding Jewish expulsion is important because, in reality, we are dealing with Venice as representing late sixteenth-century London. But of course there were Jews in London, either as Christian converts such as the ill-fated Dr Lopez, Elizabeth I's Jewish physician who was executed for supposedly plotting against the Queen's life, or among the hundred or so Jews we now assume were living openly in England – and mostly in London – at the time.

In our depiction of Shylock, we need to address a number of salient points, all of which are intrinsic not only to the construction of our image of Shylock, but to the determination of a good part of the rendering of the rest of the play. Whichever way we look at the problem, Shylock is an alien.

Despite the title of the play, it is Shylock we think of when *The Merchant of Venice* is referred to, and not Antonio. Shylock has become, through performance, the play's protagonist, rather than, as convention may demand, the antagonist to Antonio's protagonist.

Shylock is a usurer, a profession that has been attached in popular imagination to the Jew as alien. There is also a popular notion that the only profession open to Jews was that of moneylender. The situation is ambiguous, but it is important that we know what we mean in order to establish a clear picture of Shylock in his performing relationship with the other characters and how they treat him. In medieval England, as Christians were forbidden to lend money, Jews became moneylenders and were able to set high interest rates. Indeed they were, for a period of time, playing a vital role in maintaining the English treasury. However, the situation is not nearly so clear in the sixteenth century. What is evident is the fact that certain professions, notably – for this play – the law, were forbidden to Jewish people. As theatre practitioners, we need to make certain decisions regarding Shylock's role.

- If we decide that Shylock has no alternative but to adopt usury as his profession, do we have an inbuilt sympathy? Society has created him thus.
- Alternatively, if he has chosen this profession, does this not encourage a harsher view of him?
- How different is a usurer from a merchant trader? Both gamble with money. What else is the stock market?
- Is Shylock simply a vengeful man, irrespective of his Jewishness?
- Can we afford to ignore his Jewishness? Is he a bad Jew, as opposed to Jessica and Tubal who give us every reason to

suppose that they are rather better folk than many of the Christians?

- Culturally, how do we place Shylock? Do we follow the example of Laurence Olivier and make Shylock an assimilated (into the Christian culture) Jew of high nineteenth-century capitalism? Or do we follow the example of Antony Sher and represent Shylock as an oriental Jew and thus emphasize his distance, and his alienation, from Christian Venetian culture?

- Is there another representation that we may glean from the script that would work in the twenty-first century? The script tells us that Antonio was prone to spit on Shylock's Jewish gabardine.

- What is Jewish gabardine? To what extent do we draw visual imagery from the script? Cross-reference will need to be made to Portia and her male disguise as Balthazar.

We are now moving more into the territory of character representation and need to ask questions relating specifically to acting.

Character: acting conventions, including cross-gender performance

To act in the plays of Shakespeare today is to assume a task fraught with pitfalls. Apart from the ubiquity of acting conventions inherited from the late nineteenth century, and mostly associated with the name of Constantin Stanislavki and his followers under the general, and often ill-thought out, term 'Naturalism', the contemporary actor has to contend with the cultural weight and audience expectation afforded to any production of one of Shakespeare's plays. Audiences arrive at the theatre already possessing a multitude of preconceptions about how this or that character should be performed. Curiously, while Shakespeare, it is often argued, is a spirit transcendent of mere history, his works are more possessed by the theatre-going public than those of any other playwright.

To perform Shakespeare as if one were acting in a prose drama of the modern period is to deny the poetry of the theatre. Equally, to perform these dramas as if one were simply reciting poetry is to deny the theatrical life intrinsic to the drama. This kind of polarization is not particularly helpful when we realize that in any play by Shakespeare the language may move from poetry to prose from scene to scene, or even within a scene. Moreover, there will be moments when the actor is required, by the script, to be fully engaged emotionally in the character and the business of the scene, to be inside the moment, and in the next to turn on a sixpence, so to speak, and address the audience directly.

We may ask a further question by wondering to what extent a psychological approach to acting Shakespeare is appropriate? The concept, no matter how much critics assume Shakespeare to have had an intuitive sense of psychology, did not exist in the language and methods of the sixteenth and seventeenth centuries.

In the spirit of enquiry that values an understanding of the imme- diate presence of the past in our constructions of present meaning, let us consider some of the elements embedded in the scripts that reach out to the contemporary actor.

- The actors on the stage of the public playhouses were a part of a rapidly evolving theatrical practice, from the presentation of personified human qualities on the medieval stages, to the embryonic assimilation of the body and person of the actor into the fictional body of the role.
- This meant that different levels of performance had to exist simultaneously. Theatre didn't change over night and the rhetorical elements of earlier forms of acting would have remained alongside emergent forms of character presentation (Thomson, 2000, pp. 3–15).
- The audible and visible presence of the audience demanded that the actors played to that audience. A soliloquy is a very specific dramatic convention that, whichever way we perform it, disrupts the narrative flow. *Question*: Is it desirable, or even possible, for an actor to perform a soliloquy as if no one else is there to hear it? Or is a soliloquy a moment in a play when the actor shares his or her thoughts directly with the audience, recognizing also that an actor, within a soliloquy, will talk to

himself or herself. However we deal with soliloquies, we need to recognize the complexity of performance they demand.

- Apart from soliloquies, there are many instances of asides in Shakespeare's plays. For example, Shylock's speech 'How like a fawning publican he looks!' (I.iii.36–46) is an aside and should be performed to the audience, or else to whom? What implication may this carry for the audience's relationship with Shylock?

- With either a soliloquy or an aside, the actor moves aside from a full engagement with the character and adopts a liminal identity that is part character and part actor. In other words, the illusion of character is partially disrupted.

It is common knowledge that Shakespeare's plays were performed only by men and boys until the 1660s when women were first allowed to perform on the professional stage. Aside from the need to consider how boys and adolescents played the parts of women as diverse as Portia and Queen Margaret, or Rosalind and Lady Macbeth, we further need to consider the dramatic questions raised when a female character chooses to disguise herself as a male.

Adopting the clothing habits of the opposite gender in daily life was railed against from the pulpit and was, according to the records of Bridewell and the Aldermen's Court of the latter half of the sixteenth century, punishable by a variety of means. Apart from biblical prohibitions against such practices, transvestism (or cross-dressing, as we now tend to refer to the practice) formed a part of wider-reaching social transgressions relating to what one might, or might not, legally wear. For example, restrictions were placed on persons of the lower orders wearing clothing and ornaments reserved for the upper classes or the aristocracy. Women undertaking such enterprises were pilloried as prostitutes, with men condemned as betrayers of their inherent masculine status by choosing to adopt modes of effeminacy. As London was a society undergoing economic and political upheavals which threatened the previously fixed social orders, we may understand the authorities' nervousness and consequent recourse to draconian measures.

Portia is not seeking to protect herself from a threatening male

world, as are Rosalind and Viola. Her decision is more a matter of asser-
tion and potential subversion than it is of subjugation to the male
order. The early signs are manifest in her unwilling role in the execu-
tion of her dead father's will, and she adopts male dress with the aim of
rescuing Antonio from the judgment of the Court of Venice, and, in
doing so, proves her control over that particular masculine debating
chamber. Clearly her authority is ever present in Belmont, but in order
to employ her innate control in Venice, she needs to adopt male dress.
At the same time, she affords herself the opportunity to set a future
agendum for her husband through the device of the ring.

So, the actor playing Portia today should consider these questions
within the parameters set by the overall period in which we choose
to set the play.

- Portia requires a degree of signified authority in her Belmont
  manner of dress. How may we achieve this?
- How then do the clothes that Portia chooses to wear as
  Balthazar relate to her Belmont persona? She is certainly not
  one of those cross-dressing characters who cannot wield
  a sword, literal or otherwise. We may ponder on the notion
  that, in order to exercise her skill and authority, Portia, like
  Elizabeth I, has to be re-designated a man.
- We should take note of a 'clue' that might attract a modern
  actor (but one that has no legitimacy in the narrative) in Act III,
  scene iv, line 45, 'Now Balthazar, / As I have ever found thee
  honest true'. This would seem to indicate that Portia has
  affected this disguise before. Was it to enable her to undertake
  training as a lawyer?

The modern actor has to contend with a variety of traditions, as past
acting conventions are ever present in Shakespeare's plays. The
contemporary actor needs to experience a sense of the character's
psyche, while developing the skill to give full worth to the heightened language of the plays, as well as the versatility to move from
embodying a character to stepping aside into a liminal stage space
from which to make direct addresses to the audience. Above all, the
contemporary actor must tell the story.

Theatrical space

How and where the actor moves, tells the story, and establishes a relationship, of whatever kind, with the audience is partially determined by the nature of the performance space. We know that the plays were written for a performance space that was surrounded on at least three sides by the audience, that despite the possibility of an audience of three thousand everyone was near the stage action, that the actors could see (and hear) the audience, as well as being seen and heard, and that these conditions demanded a presentational style of acting. We also know that Shakespeare's plays are remarkably resilient and have been performed with great success in a variety of different performance spaces since their original conception. If we attend a performance in the Royal Shakespeare Theatre, we are confronted by the illusion of life presented broadly within the frame of a proscenium arch, which has outlived efforts of succeeding generations, particularly since the 1960s, to disrupt or break through its confines. The Elizabethan open stage invites the audience and the actor to share the moment; the proscenium arch, by confining the actors in a separate room, invites the audience to reflect upon the action in silence.

In England we have the opportunity to observe Shakespeare's plays being performed in a variety of spaces. Notably, apart from the many regional and metropolitan theatres built on nineteenth-century models, we have the examples of the Royal Shakespeare Company's main auditorium (proscenium arch), and the Swan (based on a Jacobean model) in Stratford-upon-Avon. There is also the New Globe Theatre on the South Bank in London, whose design is based on the extant evidence of late sixteenth-century playhouses.

The New Globe Theatre, while it may be considered as only an informed guess as to the architectural details of the original play-house, has alerted us to certain aspects of the performances of the time, in particular the shared interactive experience of the performers and the audience. However, the development of the Swan Theatre has, by common consent, created one of the most exciting performance spaces in the country by building the theatre around a thrust stage and an auditorium that allows every member of the audience to feel an intimate connection with the actors' performances. The Other Place theatre offered the possibility of even greater intimacy with the performances and, as a flexible space, created an opportunity for experimental work with the plays of Shakespeare's period, as well as new plays. The point to understand is that each space offers a different relationship with Shakespeare's plays. The New Globe Theatre (and indoors the Swan) can engage a modern audience in ways comparable to the engagement of Shakespeare's original audience, and that affects the text in performance. Different theatrical spaces create different aesthetic demands, and ultimately, we may argue, different meanings.

Our questions may be:

- Given that the New Globe Theatre recreates a reasonable facsimile of the original material conditions of performance, should we aim to produce Shakespeare's plays in that kind of context?
- However, we should also remember that we couldn't, even if we considered it to be desirable, recreate the social and intellectual conditions within which the original theatre was created. Moreover, would we wish all productions of Shakespeare to exist as a form of cultural memorial to an imagined original production?
- Many theatregoers expect, and even yearn for, the security of a traditional production. But what do they mean by a 'traditional' production (Goodwin, 1964, p. 41)? The Royal Shakespeare Theatre has an end-on proscenium arch stage, and despite many attempts to 'break through' the frame of the proscenium arch, the productions remain illusionistic, requiring the actors to adopt a form of acting which the audience may only witness. *The Merchant of Venice* has, of course, been staged many times in this theatre. Do we think it is the most appropriate performance space for a play that may be considered as a play of social interiority?
- The Swan Theatre is interesting in that, although its form is inspired by notions of a Jacobean indoor playhouse, it operates very much on its own terms. Here we have a performance

space that is enclosed by the auditorium on three sides, and that encourages an intimacy between the audience and the actors, but still allows for the modern imagination in theatre production. Curiously, the Swan can accommodate both epic and intimate staging.

- Is this the kind of performance space appropriate for *The Merchant of Venice*?
- Or does an even more flexible form of performance space offer greater opportunities for this play?

The development of what is commonly referred to as theatre-in-the-round, particularly in the latter half of the twentieth century, has offered performance possibilities that range from a fixed, literal, 'in-the-round' stage, through to the increasingly popular, site-specific performance space (where non-specifically designed performance spaces are adapted for the performance in question), or site-sensitive performance (where the performance develops a specific relationship to the history of the physical space).

- What might we gain by performing *The Merchant of Venice* in the round? An interesting exercise would be to envisage the same play performed in the three spaces of the Royal Shakespeare Company: the Royal Shakespeare Theatre – end-on proscenium stage; the Swan Theatre – thrust stage; and the Other Place theatre (when it was open) – flexible performance space.

We may ask ourselves the following questions regarding space.

- To what extent is a certain performance style embedded in Shakespeare's plays? Are the plays as they are (language, character relationships, movement of scenes from one place to another) because they grew with the physical performance space? In other words, is there an interdependence between the evolution of the drama and the evolution of the physical performance space?
- Are there certain kinds of performance space that lend themselves more readily than others to the kinds of dramatic

dynamic that we observe on the stages of the sixteenth century? Or are the plays endlessly adaptable? Or is meaning intrinsically bound up with physical space and convention?

Implicit stage directions and the role of the director

The role of the theatre director has evolved, in a recognizable form, since the last decades of the nineteenth century. However, what we may term the 'polemical director' is a twentieth-century phenomenon, particularly so in the latter half and now into the twenty-first century. By 'polemical' I don't mean to emphasize the aggressive aspect of the word's meaning, but more to focus attention on the controversy that is often created when a director's aim is to create an original, visionary view of a play. Occasionally, we hear more of the director's vision than we do of the writer's play. For example, we often refer to Peter Brook's *A Midsummer Night's Dream*, Peter Stein's *As You Like It*, or Giorgio Strehler's *The Tempest*. I am not arguing against the directorial vision when it emerges from the skill and artistry of men like this, but so often in lesser talents the 'vision' is imposed on the play rather than drawn out of Shakespeare's own words and stagecraft.

An alternative view is that directing in the theatre should be more about empowerment than about control; that is, empowerment of the playwright and empowerment of the actor. The extreme opposite is Edward Gordon Craig's notion of the director/designer as the controlling force in the theatre, with the actor functioning only as an *Übermarionette*.

There are two salient points to consider.

- All the people (actors, directors, electricians etc.) in a theatre have the potential to make a creative contribution to the making of the performance.
- Moreover, the playwright should not be subordinated (as is often the case) to the wishes of the other participants. Equally, the director, actors and other contributors should not be relegated to the role of merely operating as interpretative crafts-

men and women. All participants should find their voice within the process.

I have mentioned, in earlier chapters, the importance of Robert Weimann's phrase 'past significance and present meaning' when we work with Shakespeare's plays. One form of 'past significance' may be embodied within the received text/script's 'implicit stage directions', which are intrinsically related to the stagecraft of the day (Banham, 1991, pp. 269–74). As Martin Banham points out, the opening of Act V, with Lorenzo and Jessica, not only creates a mood, but also indicates the time of day. The Elizabethan audience would have accepted the convention in which a visual image, shifts of style, and tone are *heard* within the language of the characters' speeches. A modern audience, used more to the image than the word, would expect a lighting change, a change of setting, or some other visual signal, and may well have difficulty in locating the time, place or action from the heightened language.

In *Romeo and Juliet*, the young lovers' first exchange is in the form of a sonnet, where the emphasis of the theatrical moment is on what is spoken by both of them, and not on any particular action. This is an indication, to the astute actors and director, of a certain convention of playing that binds the actors by the remembrance that it would have been two boy actors in the original context. The formality of the sonnet should indicate a formal relationship of etiquette far removed from the social behaviour of modern teenagers.

Directors employ as many different methods as there are directors. Some engage in lengthy scholarly work on the chosen text and decide how they wish each scene to be formed within the overall rhythm of the play before attending the first rehearsal. Trevor Nunn as a young director is reported to have conducted early rehearsals with all the moves pre-planned, whereas actors reported that Peter Brook gave every impression, in early rehearsals of *A Midsummer Night's Dream*, of not having actually read the play. The truth of the matter is that, whether or not such claims are to be trusted, every director has to seek a personal relationship not only with the play, but also with the actors. For choice, I believe that the actors should be at the centre of the collective learning process through rehearsal, with the director taking on the role of practical seminar leader. In the end, someone has to take decisions regarding the shape and rhythm of the production, but the shaping is of material created between the playwright and the actors, and not dictated from the edge of the rehearsal room.

Interval

One final point to consider is where to place the interval if there is to be one. Some scholars have argued that the performances in the Elizabethan playhouses may have been run without a break. This invites us to wonder at the stamina of audiences of the day. Were Shakespeare's plays performed at a rapid pace that a contemporary would find hard to follow? Or were they heavily cut in performance? Alternatively, we may consider the possibility that there were breaks in the performance for musical interludes, acrobats, conjurors, or even tight-rope walkers. Few directors of recent productions have taken the bold step to perform without interval, and those who have done so have generally worked with a short play, or with a truncated Quarto.

Placing the interval in *The Merchant of Venice*:

- What is the function of an interval, apart, that is, from allowing the audience to support the variety of facilities on offer in the theatre?
- If we are to have an interval, where should it be placed?
- We also wish to contrive a situation that ensures the audience's return after the interval.
- There are two possible places in *The Merchant of Venice*: after Act III, scene iv, or possibly after Act IV, scene i. (A production in Birmingham at the Repertory Theatre in 1915 had two intervals: after Act II, scene vi, and Act III, scene iv.)
- With the former we have built to a climax, and breathing space is achieved before launching into the court scene.
- With the latter, we may lose the audience. What is there to come back for after Shylock's demise? Many leading actors

playing Shylock have been tempted by the idea of dropping the fifth Act.

The scenes in action

This second part of the chapter will take the form of a workshop discussion with the aim of leading the reader through the performance questions and possibilities inherent in the chosen text. Such a learning method is intrinsically an open pedagogic mode leading to a series of informed questions regarding the material practice of theatre, rather than the enclosure that inevitably results from proposing clear answers. The aim is to establish a four-way dialogue between author, reader, the text (which really is a script at this stage), and the range of theatrical practices in question. A spirit of openness will develop in the knowledge that theatrical texts/scripts are plural in interpretation, and our task is to discover the excitement in the range of creative decisions available to the informed reader.

I would further prosecute the case for this approach to be considered as a model for the role of the director in theatre. I am firmly of the view that the ideal model for the production of theatre is that of the ensemble, that theatre making is a collective art form. Rather than the director 'telling actors what to do', throwing each scene open to the actors in order to see what ideas are formed through free-ranging practice is an effective way by which actors may be empowered within the whole rehearsal process, and gain a deeper understanding of the material that their personages will embody. This is not to argue for a 'free for all' collective bargaining in the rehearsal room, and we may see the possibility of three stages to the rehearsal process:

1   the actors 'play' with each scene, with the director observing;
2   the actors and the director negotiate and build together on the discoveries and problems encountered by the actors;
3   the director then becomes the main problem-solver – the outside eye – even to the extent of choreographing movements, gestures, intonations and so on, but what she or he is

choreographing has been made collaboratively by the actors and the director.

Our first task in envisaging the possible performance is to find ways by which to gain an overall sense of the scene structure and the narrative rhythms that will determine the pace of the play. Elizabethan plays are written in scenes; and Acts, where they exist, are most likely to be editorial divisions, which may disrupt the rhythm of the play rather than adding structure and meaning. Admittedly, we can't always (unless a chorus is deployed) be sure where Shakespeare would have placed his 'Act' breaks, but we do know when the scene changes.

With *The Merchant of Venice*, we know that the play's action is split between Venice and Belmont, and the frequent transition of scene from Venice to Belmont provides a nightmare for the production that sets its aspiration on a full pictorial setting. The result, particularly in the nineteenth century, was that scenes were cut, merged, or re-arranged in order to meet the demands of the scenography, with the subsequent disruption of the play's dramatic tension. Peter Thomson alerts us to the purpose of Shakespeare's ordering of the scenes as they are: 'Shakespeare's strategy, perhaps his major achievement, in *The Merchant of Venice* is to create suspense through the employment of "imminence". What is about to happen in Venice or in Belmont is constantly interrupted by a shift to the other place' (Cookson and Loughrey, 1992, p. 61). If we look at a list of the scenes in order, each with its narrative objective, we will gain a sense of the story we have to tell as actors.

The scenes

I.i **Venice**. Introduction to Antonio and Bassanio. Bassanio's need to borrow money in order to reach the fabled Belmont and Portia.

I.ii **Belmont**. Introduction to Portia and Nerissa and significance of the caskets. The Prince of Morocco's arrival is imminent.

I.iii	**Venice.** Introduction to Shylock and his relationship with the Christians in general and Antonio in particular. The signing of the bond is imminent.
II.i	**Belmont.** Introduction to the Prince of Morocco. His choice of casket is imminent.
II.ii	**Venice.** Introduction to Launcelot Gobbo and his father, Old Gobbo. Launcelot's difficult decision to leave Shylock's employment and seek employment with Bassanio. Gratiano's request to go to Belmont with Bassanio reminds us of the imminent progression to Belmont. All this business may well be a device to keep the audience in suspense, as we know that Morocco is back in Belmont deliberating on his choice of casket.
II.iii	**Venice.** Introduction to Jessica, Shylock's daughter. We are given a sense of the stressful nature of the relationship between daughter and father. We are also offered further dramatic expectation in the planned elopement with Lorenzo.
II.iv	**Venice.** Planning the elopement and the knowledge that Jessica is planning to steal gold and jewels from her father. (It is worth noting that the family line in Jewish families is mostly passed on through the daughter and not the son.)
II.v	**Venice.** Shylock's house. Further develops the relationship between Jessica and Shylock.
II.vi	**Venice.** Jessica and Lorenzo elope, taking with them Shylock's gold and jewels. Bassanio's departure for Belmont is imminent.
II.vii	**Belmont.** Our first glimpse of how Portia deals with the suitors and the caskets. Morocco's fatal choice.
II.viii	**Venice.** Antonio's learning of the wreck of one of his ships is imminent.
II.ix	**Belmont.** Arragon makes his fatal choice, the scene ending with Bassanio's arrival is imminent.
III.i	**Venice.** Salerio and Solanio bait Shylock. Tubal reports on Jessica to Shylock. Antonio's ruin is imminent.

III.ii	**Belmont.** This is a crucial scene in the comedic narrative of the play. Bassanio makes the correct choice, but he leaves his wife and Belmont to attempt to avert Antonio's tragedy, which is imminent.
III.iii	**Venice.** A short scene in which Antonio's death seems imminent.
III.iv	**Belmont.** In which Portia plans an imminent departure for Venice disguised as a lawyer, with Nerissa disguised as her clerk.
III.v	**Belmont.** A curious short scene (one of a number) between Launcelot, Jessica and Lorenzo, which could be read in many ways, one of which is deeply anti-Semitic. May well have been run on from the previous scene without any clear distinction between the two.
IV.i	**Venice.** The court scene, which brings the Venetian part of the plot to its climax (as Scene 14 [Act III, scene ii] appears to bring the comedic part of the plot to its climax). A sense of dramatic imminence created by Portia's last-minute intervention of a trick based on the letter of the law.
IV.ii	**Venice.** The awkward predicament of Bassanio and Gratiano over the matter of the rings. Their discomfort when they next meet their wives, imminent.
V	**Belmont.** The comedic resolution for Bassanio and Portia, and Nerissa and Gratiano, but Antonio is left alone, just as Jessica receives the news of her father's predicament. This kind of ending appears elsewhere in Shakespeare, as we see in *Twelfth Night* with Malvolio, Antonio and, to an extent, Feste being excluded from the resolution.

As we approach each scene, we will need to outline certain information, such as the action of the scene. This will then be followed by a series of questions – generally, but not always, under the headings of 'setting', 'language', 'mood' and 'character'. However, there are two general points that must be kept in mind.

1 The rapid turn-over of scenes demands fluidity of entrances and exits by actors. If our production designs somehow impede the flow of bodies on and off stage, the dramatic narrative will suffer.

2 We need to adopt a shorthand for different forms of staging and performance space ranging from the openness of thrust and flexible spaces to the enclosure of the pictorial picture frame. I propose that we employ the two generic terms *open staging* and *enclosed staging*, which demand of the actor different ways of relating to, and communicating with, the audience. Of course, with both shapes of performance space the actors interrelate within the performance space, and the audience observes (overhears) the action. However, the difference between the two forms of staging lies in the distance of the relationship of the audience to the action. Actors within an enclosed form of staging, framed by the proscenium arch, confront the audience by acting outwards in one direction, whereas actors working in an open form of staging have audience on three or four sides of the action. The actors need then to work, as it were, in three dimensions, sharing with, rather than presenting the drama to, the audience.

ACT I

Act I, scene i

185 lines
Venice

Plot objectives

We are introduced to the merchant of the title, Antonio, and, initially, to his companions Salerio and Solanio, then to Antonio's particular friend Bassanio and two others, Gratiano (who will fall in love with Nerissa) and Lorenzo (who is in love with Jessica, Shylock's daughter).

There are two parts to the action of this scene. The first aims to inform us of Antonio's state of mind and the position of his trading fortunes (**lines 1–56**). However, this information, while it will be of use later on in the play, is secondary to our introduction to the tantalizing image of Portia and Belmont, and to Bassanio's desire (is his desire for her money or her love, or both?) (**lines 122–85**). The final lines prepare us for our first meeting with Shylock in scene iii.

Setting

How do we envisage this scene? It is the very first moment of encounter for the audience and all we are told is that the setting is Venice. So we are left with, in one sense, a blank page, but in another very significant way, a host of visual expectations about how Shakespeare's work should appear in performance.

The original setting would have been the bare thrust stage of the playhouse, so we may take this as one end of a spectrum, elements of which are easily translated into a theatre-in-the-round, or the stage of a theatre like the Swan in Stratford-upon-Avon. Both of these stages work best with the minimum of scenery and properties, placing the actor at the centre of the experience, which is, of course, apposite to our understanding of the original conditions of the performance. Certainly, we should note that this scene is written almost entirely in blank verse, containing rather high-flown rhetorical imagery that serves to inhibit any sense of intimacy between Antonio and Salerio and Solanio (not that there is any indication of that level of relationship). Later in the scene, whilst we assume there to be intimacy of some kind between Antonio and Bassanio, the language scarcely reinforces it.

At the other end of the notional scenographic spectrum, we have the possibility of the visual richness offered by pictorial scenery, which may place our scene in an artist's vision of the Rialto, or the interior of a building in Venice.

Decisions of this nature cannot be made for this scene alone, but must be made for the presentation of the whole play. So we must ask ourselves where and how we wish to place the action. Do we want to keep the staging to a minimum and rely on the language to create images in the audience's minds? Or do we think the play would be better served by scenery that gives a precise visual location to Venice and Belmont?

Action, language and actors

We have just three characters on stage at the start of the play: Antonio, Salerio and Solanio. Antonio's first speech is a remarkably low-key start to any play, let alone one that is often classed as a comedy. We learn from the first lines (**1–6**) that Antonio is in a state of melancholy.

Question:

* Is Antonio in a state of melancholy because he is ill, or because it is fashionable to be so, or perhaps because he is in love with Bassanio?

Whichever way we decide to play this part, we are dealing with a rather ineffectual character whose centrality in the play's title is casually usurped by Shylock and Portia.

The language of the scene, as we have already noted, gives a number of clues to its mood and playing style.

Lines 1–56 are taken up with Antonio's melancholy and Salerio and Solanio's attempts to settle Antonio's mind, which is 'tossing on the ocean'. Two speeches (**lines 15–23 and 24–40**), despite the overblown language, do take us right into the world of mercantile Venice, but in a curious manner. It is rare to find, particularly in the 1590s, trade described in such language. It seems to be a meeting between two different worlds: the imagery of an older world, with the subject matter of the then modern mercantile world. However, Antonio, despite his self-absorption in melancholy, is able to reassure us that he would not be so foolish as to trust all his ventures to one vessel: 'My ventures are not in one bottom trusted' (**line 42**).

Solario then suggests that Antonio must be in love (**line 46**). This seems to hit the bone and it is worth reading the editor's note (n. 46) in our text, where the editor suggests that Antonio's ambiguous response is 'an exclamation of reproach rather than a clear negative'

(Brown, 1967, p. 7). This is a vital moment for the actor playing Antonio, for he must, in some way, change his intonation and gestural qualities in order to refute the suggestion. It is a moment of minor dramatic tension that also signals a more important shift in the scene with Bassanio's arrival.

There follows a brief interlude and exchange with the newcomers, in which we learn that Bassanio, Gratiano and Lorenzo are clearly closer in their friendship to Antonio than are Salerio and Solanio. As directors and actors we must be prepared for a change in tempo.

In this interlude, the actor playing Gratiano must establish his persona and presence. He talks too much and to little effect. This will degenerate into vehement bluster in the court scene and we need to establish the level at which we will pitch Gratiano. Is he a talkative but essentially harmless character, or is there another level of vindictiveness and racism to be developed by the actor?

Once Gratiano and Lorenzo have left the stage, we reach the real point of the scene, which has to be held by two actors on stage. Are we to devise ways in which only two actors in a fairly intimate scene may hold the focus and attention of the audience, or should we consider ways of 'filling the stage'?

As with Gratiano, we need to establish the level at which to pitch Bassanio: is he a well-meaning but inadequate youth who has failed to live within his means, but who does possess a genuine friendship (of whatever kind) for Antonio? Or is he a fairly calculating wastrel who has squandered his own and a good part of Antonio's money, and now has set his sights on a rich and beautiful woman?

Again the language is excessively decorous and studded with classical references. The reference to Brutus's wife Portia is fine, given the sterling qualities of that woman, and offers a hint at high-status playing for the actor of Portia. But the reference to Portia of Belmont as the Golden Fleece sought by Jason/Bassanio portrays Portia as a commodity to be achieved, rather than a relationship to be reinforced – an image that is further developed by the binding of Portia to the caskets by her father's will. We might also wish to remember that, if Bassanio is likened to Jason and Portia is to take on the role of Medea, the love interest in the myth, it should be noted that Jason treated Medea pretty shabbily in later life. To develop the Golden

Fleece image further, we might also consider the implications of associating the romance-imbued mythological rite of passage that is the Jason myth with Venetian mercantile trade.

This should be an intimate scene between these two friends, but it is inevitable that certain tensions will need to be established by the actors.

- How is the actor playing Antonio to react to Bassanio wanting more money from him?
- And how is he further to react to Bassanio's wanting the money to win a rich bride? Does Portia threaten the level of intimacy between Antonio and Bassanio?

We are left anticipating a meeting with this 'fabled' woman who lives on the 'beautiful hill'.

Act I, scene ii

128 lines
Belmont

Plot objectives

The important objectives of this scene are to introduce us to Portia and the predicament in which she is placed by the terms of her father's will, as well as to provide clues to her character through her observations on the current crop of suitors. Do we take these derogatory descriptions of the Neapolitan Prince, the County Palatine, the French Lord, the English Baron, the Scottish Lord and the Duke of Saxony's nephew as examples of Portia's wit, or her xenophobia? We are also introduced to Nerissa, whose relationship with Gratiano will feature in a sub-plot. The memory of Portia's meeting with Bassanio is recalled, but thoughts of him are disrupted by the imminent arrival of the Prince of Morocco.

Setting

We are now in Belmont. All we are given by way of setting in our edition is *Belmont*, and variously in other textual editions there are references to the three caskets, gold, silver and lead, being set out in a room in Portia's house. How are we, the audience, transported to this fabled place? Remember, the only knowledge we have of Belmont and Portia is derived from Bassanio's reference to the Golden Fleece. If our staging is pictorial and enclosed, a substantial set change will have had to take place. If our staging is open and less reliant on complex stage machinery, easy and fluid movement between scenes may be achieved. However, whereas the Elizabethan audience would have found little difficulty in making this leap of the imagination, a modern audience more used to the visual placing of events would find the transition less easy.

We should also note that we have few clues as to what kind of place Belmont is, other than the meaning of the name and Bassanio's fantasizing in Act I, scene i.

Action, language and actors

As with Antonio, we are introduced to Portia in a very low-key manner: 'By my troth Nerissa, my little body is aweary of this great world' (**lines 1–2**). Why is it that two of the most significant figures in the play are introduced in such a lacklustre mood; hardly a sure way to energize the audience's attention to a leading character?

While the function here is scene-setting for the events to come in the play, it also gives us our first clues to the character of Portia. Her reactions to Nerissa's references to the current round of suitors leave us in no doubt as to the fact that here we have no easily acquiescent meek heroine, but one who is quick of wit (or does she simply reveal her prejudice against men of certain cultures?), and one who is not finding the constraints laid upon her an easy burden. Portia's responses to each of the suitors contrast with the seeming acquiescence of her first two lines.

So how does the actor playing Portia deal with this tension, and establish her presence on the stage and as mistress of Belmont? **Lines 1–37** are worth investigating, but first we need to make some general observations regarding the language in this scene. Unlike the previous scene, this one is written in prose, with the eccentric exception of the doggerel couplet of the last two lines, 'Come Nerissa, sirrah go before: / Whiles we shut the gate upon one wooer, another knocks at the door.' Whereas Antonio's mood and Bassanio's ambitions are wrapped in extravagant imagery, Portia's dismissals of her clustered suitors are delivered in the most straightforward of prose.

Nerissa's reminding her mistress that she is actually fortunate, at least in her social and material position, if not her freedom, elicits a response that demonstrates an almost lawyer-like reasoning. Portia, by **lines 20–1**, retreats from this 'reasoning' by reminding herself that choice is a limited commodity in her own case. Portia and Nerissa then spend the rest of the scene with the one presenting each suitor, and the other dismissing them in the most peremptory fashion.

Again, with just two actors filling the stage, establishing a presence is all-important. Portia must move from her brief melancholy to self-examination, and on to the suitor's dismissal. At **line 114**, do we perceive a need for a momentary pause, a wistful reflection on the memory of Bassanio in the lines, 'I remember him well, and I remember him worthy of thy praise'? However, she (the actor) must prepare for an abrupt break of that moment's mood with the imminent arrival of the Prince of Morocco. We may put aside textual questions arising around the sudden appearance of the single doggerel couplet and consider the opportunity afforded to the actor playing Portia to break away from her moment's reflection on the memory of Bassanio. The doggerel couplet is not inconsistent with the off-hand dismissal of the suitors in the preceding dialogue, and the rough rhythms of the couplet sit easily on an actor's tongue, allowing her to sweep from the stage to deal with the matter of the business at hand.

Act I, scene iii

177 lines
Venice

Plot objectives

The scene has been set for the Portia and Bassanio plot to develop, but first the loan must be achieved. At a simple narrative level, the purpose of this scene is to introduce the audience to Shylock, and to explain the nature of the bond that is to act as surety for Shylock's loan to Antonio. At a more complex level, much more is happening by way of indicating Venetian and Christian attitudes towards foreigners, and Shylock in particular, as well as offering more information on Antonio's character. We will discuss these aspects of the scene and what the actors may need to bear in mind in the third section of our discussion of Act I, scene iii.

There is clear and undisputed personal tension between Shylock and Antonio, with, it would seem, Antonio being the main aggressor. We may cite **lines 101–24** as evidence of Antonio's regular public insults to Shylock, because of his supposed 'Jewish' occupation, calling him 'misbeliever' because of his Jewish faith, spitting on his Jewish gabardine, spitting in his face, and kicking him as one would a dog. Antonio does not deny any of this and, moreover, indicates that he would willingly repeat his behaviour. His rationale at this point (**lines 125–32**) is to propose that Shylock lends the money, not in kindness, but to his enemy, so that, 'thou may'st with better face / Exact the penalty'. Now we have the scene set for Shylock to justify in his own mind setting a trap for Antonio.

We leave this important scene in the play's development with a reminder of the concern in scene 1 with the potential disasters that may occur when all one's vessels are at sea. The signing of the bond is imminent.

Setting

We are back in Venice in the blinking of an eye, and we may imagine Portia exiting with her couplet at the end of scene 2, as Bassanio and Shylock enter to set up scene 3. Venice, in one sense or another, appears before our eyes, or in our collective hearing. On an open stage, whether in the original context of Shakespeare's theatre, or on a present-day stage, we may speculate on the theatrical effect of the opening line, 'Three thousand ducats, well', being delivered on the move as Shylock and Bassanio enter, a split second after Portia's flourish of a couplet has been delivered. As an aside, it is worth speculating on the theatrical possibilities of people seeming to be constantly on the move as the narrative drives forward. For the most part, short scenes, moving from place to place, create a sense of urgency, matched by the growing sense of urgency within individual scenes, such as the tension when a casket is about to be chosen, or the urgency of outcome within the trial scene.

Action, language and actors

We must approach this scene with care. Apart from the necessary business of the agreeing of the loan and the nature of the bond, first and foremost it is the moment when we meet Shylock. The practical questions fall thick and fast and it is worth pausing for a moment to consider the implications of Shylock's physical, social and cultural presence on our stage.

Physical bodies populate a stage, and what may be alluded to in words on the page becomes, in production, a physical presence. Moreover any physical presence within the 'frame' of a performance is not culturally devoid of meaning. Our bodies in daily life are simultaneously physically and culturally constructed by gender, race, social status and so on, but in performance those bodies, with all their daily inscriptions, must become, as Eugenio Barba describes it, an 'extra-daily body or technique' (Barba, 1981, p. 11). The extra-daily technique or body is that which is consciously constructed through training, and directed towards specific purposes in the context of a performance. This applies to all characters on stage, and we may wish to consider what inscriptions have been carried through time when we remember that the part of Portia was written for an adolescent male actor. Do any residues of that context remain to be carried through in the character's language and actions? However, when we consider the case of Shylock, we have another layer of inscriptions to understand, inscriptions which will inform the production's political relationship to the character. We know well enough the Venetians' attitudes, but what are ours?

Any production of *The Merchant of Venice* has to make a decision as to the representation of Shylock. We have observed in Chapters 4 and 5 the variations offered by past stage readings of the play and we have seen, in recent decades, both the assimilated (westernized) Jew and the 'oriental' Jew. Whichever extra-daily body we choose for Shylock, we must recognize at the heart of the play (and despite the title, the play has become Shylock's) a racially and ethnically 'other' body. Otherness in the cultural sense means, *ipso facto*, a marginalized body, and in the case of Shylock, one which is also violated and made grotesque, the fact of which is amply borne out by this scene and Antonio's past and present behaviour towards Shylock.

The actor's problem is how to manifest this physical and psychic presence. This scene offers many interesting dramatic devices, in particular the first clear indication of direct address to the audience by Shylock. The language of the scene is mixed between prose and blank verse, with the latter form dominating. Shylock's first long speech to Bassanio, before Antonio's entrance, is in prose and, with its strange sense of violent wit, places Shylock at the centre of the stage's discourse. But when we come to the soliloquy, 'How like a fawning publican he looks' (**lines 36–47**), the scene shifts to blank verse. The actor must make a number of decisions as to how to deliver this, while remembering that more effect may be achieved by changing positions, both linguistically and gesturally, from direct address to the audience to reference back to the other characters within the fiction of the scene.

A technical point on addressing the audience is useful. So often, when actors attempt to address the audience directly, they lose a real sense of inclusion or of conspiracy with them. Often this is, in part, due to the unsympathetic architecture of the enclosed proscenium stage, within which there is a temptation to deliver the soliloquy as a general address over the heads of the audience members. The craft is in picking on various people in the audience, looking them directly in the eye and talking to them as individuals, changing focus as the rhythm of the speech demands. Curiously, this technique of direct address to individuals encompasses the rest of the audience more effectively than a general address.

We may note that the dialogue between Bassanio and Shylock, up to Antonio's entrance (**lines 1–34**), is in prose, but thereafter until the end of the scene it is, for the most part, in blank verse. What questions arising from the changes in language should be asked in relationship to performance modes? An interesting exercise for any actor is to read through the speeches and imagine where the focus of delivery is at any given moment: is it on the audience or on the other characters in the scene?

With the signing of the bond imminent, Antonio and Bassanio leave the stage with Antonio's final hypocritical shot (to Bassanio or to the audience?), 'Hie thee gentle Jew. [*to Shylock's back on his exit*] / The Hebrew will turn Christian, he grows kind.' And after Bassanio's anxiety expressed in **line 175**, Antonio's minor hubris is carried on a couplet, 'Come on, in this there can be no dismay, / My ships come home a month before the day [*The loan repayment day*].'

ACT II

Act II, scene i (scene 4)

46 lines
Belmont

Plot objectives

Back to Belmont, as Bassanio and Antonio exit from the Rialto! The Prince of Morocco arrives and his choice is imminent, but he is also made aware of the penalty for failure in **lines 39–42**. In this scene the intention is to use the caskets and the failure to make the correct choice to build the suspense in advance of Bassanio's keenly anticipated arrival.

Setting

We will need to give some thought to the various ways in which the caskets are presented on stage. Are they ever physically present when we are in Belmont? Or are they brought on when and as appropriate by some device: a trolley, or carried on by servants? How big are they? There have been productions where they are large and descend from the flies as a kind of *deus ex machina*. They may fulfil some overt symbolic purpose, or they may be small and merely functionary and sit on Portia's desk. If the choice is to imbue them with some value other than the commodity value of Portia's dowry or the intrinsic value of gold, silver, and lead, what is it to be?

Action, language and actors

Morocco is the latest in the long line of suitors who, it would seem, could well have been dismissed with the sharp edge of Portia's wit. Morocco, however, is intent on impressing Portia with his courage and wealth (this puts him in a different material league from Bassanio!). However, Morocco's rhetoric in these early speeches (all in blank verse) is concerned with proving that his blood signifies courage and virility 'despite' the fact that he is black. Portia's response, which may be read as an attempt to compliment Morocco, only serves to reveal her racist attitude – you may, despite the fact that you are black, be as good 'As any comer I have look'd on yet / for my affection' (**lines 21–2**). For all the many attempts to gloss over the attitudes revealed, by arguing that Portia's remarks are more to do with the Elizabethan fashion for pale skins and the attractiveness of being 'fair-skinned', it is how the play's meaning reads now that is important.

Morocco can be played as a devastatingly attractive man and, as Trevor Nunn's television adaptation demonstrated, Portia may be made to appear to be quite taken by his sexual magnetism. A point for the actor playing Morocco to think on! Without doubt, this is one way to make a mark on stage and, with the connivance of the rest of the company, to create the possibility of a minor disruption in the general expectation of the plot. We leave them with the choice of casket imminent.

Act II, scene ii (scene 5)

Lines 197
Venice

Plot objectives

The next five scenes are unusual in that they all take place in Venice, while back in Belmont Morocco is having dinner and considering his choice of caskets. We are introduced to the clown Launcelot Gobbo, possibly one of the least amusing clowns in all of Shakespeare's plays. His main function is to act as a confidant to Jessica. We know that Morocco is about to choose the casket that will seal his fate, and the introduction of the clown is a device by which to relieve tension by diverting our attention to the trick Launcelot plays on his sand-blind father Old Gobbo. (Alternatively, it could be argued that the scene's function is to actually maintain the tension of the Morocco scene. It is one of those decisions a director must be clear about.) Launcelot's desire to leave Shylock's service in favour of Bassanio is a further useful plot device by which he will, we later find out, be able to keep in close contact with Jessica.

An interesting point of irony is that the two significant moments that move the plot along in this scene both involve people with suits to beg of Bassanio: Launcelot to leave the service of Shylock and become Bassanio's servant, and Gratiano to travel with Bassanio to Belmont. Does this adjust Bassanio's status in our eyes? After all, until now we have seen him only in the role of supplicant to Antonio and Shylock (and, potentially, to Portia).

Setting

Although we are clearly back in Venice, the setting of this scene is not specifically of any great importance. We assume that we are, or how else does Launcelot come upon his father fresh from the country and wandering the streets of Venice in search of his son? The comings and goings of various folk in this scene, with their suits to Bassanio, would be served by the fluidity of a bare stage, or by a setting that indicates the regular flow of human traffic.

Action, language and actors

There are moments with Shakespeare's clowns that offer interesting staging problems and possibilities, and despite my view that Launcelot Gobbo is one of the least interesting of the type, we have in this scene the possibility of an interesting interface between 'then and now' (remembering again Robert Weimann's phrase, 'past significance and present meaning') in Gobbo's address to the audience (**lines 1–30**). In present-day terms this speech may be equated with the performance of stand-up comedy. The stage direction in our copy of the text signals the fact that Launcelot is alone on the stage, and unless he is to undertake the unlikely task of talking to himself for the whole speech he is performing *with* the audience in the manner of the stand-up act today. One of the fascinating elements in stand-up routines and the telling of complicated stories is the way in which the performer must change roles and narrative functions within the same performance. At one moment the performer is the narrator, the next s/he is a character; often more than one character in the story. This technique of performance, which, by its very nature, breaks theatrical illusion, is illustrative of what I mean by the performer occupying a liminal space within performance. There are moments when the actor moves from 'being' a character to narrating the character or a moment in the narrative. Launcelot tells us the situation as our narrator, then shifts position to be 'the fiend', then moves on to becoming his own conscience. We have the same performer/actor throughout, but playing many parts. Moreover, once audiences understand this convention of playing, they and the performer enter into a delightful conspiracy of dialogue. Another example, which while it does not require the multiple playing of this Gobbo speech, does engage the audience in a conspiracy that questions illusion and reality, is Bottom's speech delivered to the audience on being awakened from his 'dream' (*A Midsummer Night's Dream*, IV.i.198–215).

The rest of the scene, mostly in prose, but with interpolations of blank verse, particularly in the exchange between Bassanio and Gratiano, is straightforward.

Act II, scene iii (scene 6)

22 lines
Venice

Plot objectives

This is the first appearance of Jessica, Shylock's daughter. Her relationship with Lorenzo is the second of the three male/female love relationships in the play and emotionally (and perhaps politically in the present day) more important than the Gratiano and Nerissa pairing. In this scene we are introduced to her planned elopement with Lorenzo, her complex and distressing relationship with her father ('But though I am a daughter to his blood / I am not to his manners'), and the prospect that she will (willingly?) renounce her Jewish faith to become a Christian. This latter point would have been a perfectly respectable, even desirable, notion to the Elizabethan audience, but what of a present-day audience's reception?

Setting

Although the stage direction locates this scene only in Venice, we may assume that it takes place inside Shylock's house. All of these Venice scenes (ii–vii) are short 'frames' offering necessary information while delaying our discovery of the outcome of Morocco's fate. What is required in staging is the ability to move easily and freely from moment to moment. In this, any consideration regarding setting must be subordinated to the actors and the need to focus on what is being said, the contrasting moods of the Shylock/Jessica relationship and the emerging anticipation and excitement of the revellers in planning the elopement of Jessica and Lorenzo.

Action, language and actor

The tasks set for Jessica and Launcelot are demanding despite the fact that the scene can only last a few minutes. The actor playing Jessica must establish herself very quickly – she is no passing figure and must play a significant part in the events at sub-plot level. How does she establish her identity in 15 lines (**1–9 and 15–21**)? Launcelot, after his 'stand-up comedy' routine and the fairly meaningless trick he plays on his father, now must demonstrate a close and trusting relationship – albeit as a servant – with Jessica. The actor must negotiate the trust while appearing to exhibit the 'accepted' attitude towards marginal people (non-Christians, 'most beautiful pagan, most sweet Jew', a back-handed compliment if there ever was one).

Act II, scene iv (scene 7)

39 lines
Venice

Plot objectives

The preparation for the masque (carnival) and Jessica and Lorenzo's elopement.

Setting

Necessarily the street, but how should we indicate this? We know that it is 'four of clock' (**line 8**) and that they have 'two hours'. The scene also signals the fact that Shylock is now prepared to dine with Antonio and Bassanio.

Action, language and actors

The one speech that demands our attention is Lorenzo's (**lines 29–39**). Here the actor must impart information that is useful, such as the method by which the elopement is to be achieved, and that Jessica is to bring with her gold and jewels from her father's house. More importantly, what emerges is the hint of religion and redemption preparing us for Jessica's 'willing' conversion to Christianity and Shylock's enforced conversion.

Act II, scene v (scene 8)

56 lines
Venice

Plot objectives

The point of this scene is to confirm the relationship between Jessica and Shylock and to build the audience's anticipation of Jessica and Lorenzo's planned elopement. (Has the audience by now lost interest in Morocco's fate?) The details of Shylock and Jessica's relationship will be dealt with in detail under the heading of 'Action, language and actors'.

Setting

[*Venice before Shylock's House*] is interesting if we are to take the stage direction in our text (p. 49) as accurate. We might assume that it tells us much about the original performance conditions. 'Before Shylock's house': why not inside it? On the stage of the Elizabethan theatre there would not have been any attempt at the scenographic illusion of a Venetian interior, so in order to facilitate the smooth transition of one scene to another all that is needed is the words of the scene to provide the setting.

Action, language and actors

Although it is far from obvious in Shylock's speech (**lines 11–18**) to Jessica, it is possible to play this as a moment of near-tenderness between Shylock and his daughter. Yes there is a clear degree of malignity in Shylock's words; but let us not forget the kind of treatment he has had to endure from Antonio. We must also consider what is implied by the knowledge that Shylock is now to dine with Antonio and Bassanio, after vowing in scene iii, **lines 29–34**, never to eat with them. If the moment is played in a way that reveals some humanity in his relationship with his daughter, we gain the opportunity to create a dramatic tension between this moment and Shylock's next speech (**lines 28–39**) when he rails against the 'shallow fopp'ry' of the Christian youths. There is much of the puritan about Shylock that has more depth to it than the simple designation of miserliness.

Act II, scene vi (scene 9)

68 lines
Venice

Plot objectives

Amidst the confusion of the carnival, Jessica and Lorenzo elope, taking with them a considerable amount of Shylock's gold and jewels. May we pause and consider that the jewels may well have been Jessica's mother's jewels? What does this say about our understanding of Jessica and Shylock's relationship? Bassanio's departure for Belmont is imminent.

Setting

Again, we should assume that the placing of this scene is vaguely out of doors, but with the addition of the stage direction in our copy, on Jessica's entrance, '[*Enter*] JESSICA *above* [, *in boy's clothes*]'. Inasmuch as such directions are useful for our contemporary theatre, we may assume that *above* refers to an upper level – a minstrels' gallery? – that was available to the actors in the Elizabethan theatre. Of course, in a present-day theatre, the term 'above' could mean 'up stage', derived from our general use of the terms, from the actor's standpoint, 'up stage', 'down stage', 'stage left', 'stage right' and so on, which indicate an actor's position rather like the points of a compass.

The stage direction 'above' raises many interesting possibilities for staging strategies in the Elizabethan theatre. Juliet's 'balcony' in *Romeo and Juliet*, for instance, is never referred to as a balcony, but we infer a balcony from the stage direction '*Enter Juliet aloft*'. *Antony and Cleopatra* is even more intriguing in its siting of Cleopatra's monument (Act IV, scene xvi), '*Enter Cleopatra* [*and her maids aloft*], *with* Charmian *and* Iras'; even more so when Antony appears, dying after his bungled suicide, and '*They heave Antony aloft to Cleopatra*'. Where is *aloft* sited? Is it the minstrels' gallery? Perhaps he is 'heaved' from the floor of the pit onto the stage, or could it even be from the stage onto one of the balconies in the auditorium of the theatre?

The digression to consider the use of the term 'aloft' in other plays of the period is useful in that it adds to our sense of the stagecraft that may have been employed in the original productions. Understanding such aspects of the Elizabethans' stagecraft can only add alternative dimensions to the currently accepted practices that have evolved from nineteenth-century theatre.

Action, language and actors

Shakespeare, cleverly, keeps reminding us of ships and weather in Gratiano's long-winded speech (**lines 8–19**) in which he queries Lorenzo's lateness, 'For lovers ever run before the clock' (**line 4**). It seems that ships in storms at sea, trade, and lovers' elopements all run together before the wind, and all run the risk of disaster. If we hold for a moment that complex and unlikely combination of images, we may wonder how these images relate to our characters on stage. Storms in Shakespeare often emanate from some law being broken (think of *King Lear* when the raging of the elements seems to mirror the break-up of his kingdom). In *The Merchant of Venice* the elements of nature and human sexual love are brought together in an unusual combination with mercantile trade. That they are bound together makes this play of Shakespeare's more embedded in his own developing early modern society than many of his other works. Ships being wrecked at sea and the vagaries of love have little to do with natural patterns and cycles in this very 'modern' play.

The actor playing Jessica must take serious note of the business of her donning male attire for a disguised escape. This is an added form of protection on carnival night, but for a young Jewish woman the agony of committing an act that must come near to breaking an article of faith must be double that of Portia and Nerissa, who seem to give not a second thought to acquiring a male disguise. This can only add to the stressful situation of leaving her father's house, despite its being an unhappy place in which to live. Her agony is intensified by the 'light' that must be shone upon her 'shames' (**line 41**) through her being Lorenzo's torchbearer.

Act II, scene vii (scene 10)

79 lines
Belmont

Plot objectives

After the sequence of events in Venice – our introduction to Launcelot Gobbo and his father; the introduction to Jessica; planning the elopement and the knowledge that Jessica is intending to steal gold and jewels from her father; establishing the relationship between Jessica and Shylock; Jessica and Lorenzo's final elopement, taking with them Shylock's gold and jewels; with Bassanio's imminent departure for Belmont – we eventually return to Belmont. Portia and Morocco have meanwhile dined and Morocco is about to make his fatal choice. We also have our first glimpse of how Portia deals with the suitors and the caskets.

Setting

We assume that the probability is that the casket scenes are played indoors, although there is no real reason why this should be so. What is more important is the way in which we choose to present the caskets. We have noted before that this may be achieved in a business-like (naturalistic) manner, where they are little more than desk accoutrements, or they may play a more symbolic role in which they 'perform' as a *deus ex machina*.

The way we choose to employ the caskets must fit with our overall concept of the production, all the while remembering that there is an in-built tension in the play between the seemingly modern world of mercantile commerce and the contrasting pastoral sense we have of Belmont.

Action, language and actors

The actor who is to play Morocco has a difficult task ahead of him (we assume that a male actor will generally be the choice for this part, although, of course, there is no reason at all why we have to be gender specific in our casting, as long as we establish a convention that the audience will be able to perceive and adjust to).

The scene is very much Morocco's and a lot of what happens here will depend on how we have chosen to represent him in his earlier scene (remember that there is the potential to play him as a dashing and sexually attractive male). The choice itself takes 54 lines (**4–10 and 13–60**) and continues a pattern that may be read as empty boasting or acceptable bravado. Whichever way, the actor has to be able to deal with the final rejection. Do we want to sympathize with him, or not?

The references to Portia can only serve to increase our sense of the divide between the world of Belmont and the world of Venice. In particular, we need to look carefully at **lines 38–47**. How does this image of Portia match with the young lawyer Balthazar? Are these suitors, Arragon as well as Morocco, from worlds so totally divorced from the commerce of Venice? Are we to take them seriously at all? Is Shakespeare using them as comic light relief? (We don't get much indication of that in the text from Launcelot Gobbo, but, of course, we don't know how much of it is a part that invited the clown [Will Kemp?] to play *away* from the text for light relief.) If we do accept the playing of the suitors as light relief, we must not forget that the consequences of their choosing correctly are serious for Portia. Perhaps we may consider the notion that the clue to playing these casket scenes is not so much in Morocco's performance as it is in Portia's reaction to his or Arragon's performance. This will lay great responsibility on the actor playing Portia for, while not being the obvious focus of the scene, she must draw attention from Morocco to just the right degree to affect the mood of the scene.

This scene also carries one of those awkward lines that everyone thinks that they know, '*All that glisters is not gold.*' This is usually misquoted as 'All that glitters is not gold,' and its very familiarity makes it difficult for any actor to speak it without appearing forced. We may be pretty certain that an audience armed with the knowledge that the line is coming up soon will wait in anticipation. This is one of the pitfalls of performing Shakespeare, and Portia will have a whole speech in the trial scene that carries an even greater level of expectation. Does the actor throw the line away, frame it by emphasizing it, or what?

The scene ends with a couplet that will, without doubt, be read as racist by a present-day audience.

> A gentle riddance, – draw the curtains, go, –
> Let all of his complexion choose me so.
>
> (lines 78–9)

Should the actor play this line directly to the audience? To her assembled servants (Nerissa may be there, or not; she is not named)? Morocco has left the scene before the couplet is spoken. Whichever way we choose, it has to be delivered so as not to disrupt the rapid and smooth flow into the next scene. Perhaps it is a throwaway line delivered over her shoulder to the audience as she leaves the stage. This may diffuse some of the impact if we wish to retain sympathy for Portia.

Act II, scene viii (scene 11)

54 lines
Venice

Plot objectives

We learn of Shylock's distress. Is he distressed more by the loss of his daughter, or by the loss of his gold? Antonio is imminently to learn of a vessel's foundering. This scene is a two-hander between Salerio and Solanio, and it is really no more than an information-giving scene. However, as we will discuss later, there are different levels of information to be gleaned, as well as recognizing that, for the actors playing Salerio and Solanio, it is their moment on stage.

Setting

Again the setting could be anywhere and nowhere. Salerio and Solanio could as well be in the street or publicly indoors in a café, or they could be privately indoors in a house. The only decision is to determine how private the conversation is. This will, to an extent, fix the level of intonation and the gestural qualities of the actors as well as the setting they occupy. The conversation could, of course, be private and intimate, but they must include the audience in the intimacy. The only agreement needed is a clear statement of convention regarding enclosed or open staging at the start of rehearsals.

Action, language and actors

On a broad interpretative level, the characterization in this scene serves to reinforce the general animosity felt by the Venetians (Christians) towards Shylock. The enjoyment in mocking Shylock's loss is clear. However, we may wish to consider distancing Salerio and Solanio from the other Venetians if we want to retain a degree of sympathy for Antonio and Bassanio. Or we may decide that they are all tarred with the same brush. This level of discussion, from the outset, is a vital element in the working relationship between director and actors.

Salerio's speech (**lines 35–49**) signals an important change of mood in the scene, from insensitive mockery to one of introspective concern for Antonio, and sets the scene for a sense of Antonio's disaster as imminent. **Lines 46–9** demonstrate more than just a passing comment, for they raise our awareness of the depth of feeling (just friendship, or otherwise) that Antonio bears for Bassanio, and offer a clue to how their parting may well have been performed, as well as to how we may wish to develop the performance of Antonio's character.

Lines such as these are important illustrations of how actors can work together as an ensemble, passing around information about each other. Information imparted for the benefit of the audience can also provide clues to actors on how to interpret given moments in the text.

Act II, scene ix (scene 12)

101 lines
Belmont

Plot objectives

Arragon makes his fatal choice, and the scene ends with Bassanio's arrival imminent. Is this simply another information scene? Or is it fulfilling some other purpose within the dramatic structure? First of all it offers the audience another glimpse of the caskets and contender for Portia's hand in marriage, but it is also part of the dramatic 'build-up' to Bassanio's arrival. However, we don't know whether Bassanio will make the correct choice. Perhaps it will be the Prince of Arragon. Arragon is often performed as an effete fool, and of course he does choose the silver casket with the 'portrait of a blinking idiot' (**line 54**) inside it. It is useful for us to know that Ar(r)agon (the usual spelling is with a single 'r') was an ancient and powerful kingdom in north-eastern Spain, and given the political tensions between Spain and England in the sixteenth century, it is quite possible that the portrayal of Arragon as a fool was a deliberate piece of political satire at the expense of an enemy.

We end the scene with the imminent arrival of Bassanio; at least we assume that the young Venetian so highly praised by a messenger announcing his arrival is Bassanio (**lines 86–95**). Of course the messenger could well be in the pay of Bassanio and sent ahead to lay the foundations for his suit. Would this make us more or less sympathetic to Bassanio?

Setting

For the sake of visual consistency we must repeat the decision made in the tenth scene (Act II, scene vii). We do have in this scene a reference to the drawing of the curtain (**line 1**). This clue may lead us to assume that in the original context the 'inner stage', if such a location existed in any of the Elizabethan playhouses, would have been the obvious site for the caskets, allowing them to be revealed and hidden by the simple drawing of a curtain. This historical possibility is interesting, but in no way should it prevent the employment of the caskets in a more symbolic way.

Action, language and actors

Arragon speaks ornately, though with uncertain control of the iambic pentameter: there is occasional slippage into extra syllables. There may, then, be good reason for playing him as a fool in order to release the audience's urge to laugh. Does this scene demand the reversal of focus that was proposed in the tenth scene, where the scene was as much governed by Portia's silent reactions to Morocco as it was by his performance? Here we may decide that the focus must be on Arragon, and allow Portia to fade into the background. Once Arragon has left the stage, we may then bring Portia back into focus, with the hoped-for arrival of Bassanio imminent.

ACT III

Act III, scene i (scene 13)

120 lines
Venice

Plot objectives

Salerio and Solanio act as narrators, giving the audience the necessary knowledge of events which will drive the narrative development. But this scene is much more. It is a scene of transition whose emotional pitch gives an added urgency to the narrative.

Antonio's ship has been 'wracked on the narrow seas' (**line 3**), the Goodwin Sands in the English Channel (this was thought possible in Act II, scene viii). On receiving this news, Shylock prepares to enforce the bond. The good news and the bad news alternate for him. From his friend Tubal he receives snippets of disheartening information about his daughter Jessica, but also news that another of Antonio's ships has been lost near Tripoli (spelt Tripolis in our text) in North Africa. This is our first meeting with Tubal and, despite the brevity of his part in the text (just this scene), he is often introduced into the trial scene as a silent observer of the events and may, by whatever reaction he gives to the events, colour our reaction to Shylock's actions.

Shylock confronts Salerio and Solanio in the certain knowledge that they are implicated in Jessica's elopement, and this only serves to intensify the antagonism between Shylock and his Christian tormentors.

The scene ends as, with Antonio's imminent ruin virtually assured, Shylock sends Tubal for an officer to arrange the arrest of Antonio.

Setting

The opening line of Solanio's, 'What news on the Rialto?', suggests that we are in a public gathering place where different folk come across each other in their day's traffic. Probably an exterior setting.

Action, language and actors

Much of this scene is delivered in prose, which is unusual for major speeches, particularly Shylock's. What implications does this carry for the way in which the scene as a whole, and in particular Shylock's major speeches, should be performed? Without doubt, this scene is one that, really for the first time in the play, carries high emotion. If the emotion is to retain shape and maintain communication with the audience, it needs, in some way, to be framed. One of the advantages of blank verse, and, indeed, any poetic use of language, is that it offers to the actor a controlling device correlative to the emotion. It is not always easy to achieve this level of discipline with prose, where the impetus may be towards the illusion that 'this is really happening'. So we need to bear in mind that we are not living this emotion, we are performing it. While we want the emotion to have substance and integrity of passion, we still have to communicate it to the audience. So what is happening in this scene?

The first point to note is that the initial exchange between Salerio and Solanio, and Shylock, depends on word-play. The word-play helps to build a sense of Shylock's state of mind, but is a controlled pathway to the emotional height of the scene; we are not launched straightaway into high emotion. There are several clear instances of this 'framing' word-play.

- Shylock knows well enough that they had some part in enabling Jessica's elopement (**lines 22–3**).

- Salerio taunts Shylock with the lines (**24–5**) that 'I (for my part) knew the tailor that made the wings she flew withal.'
- Solanio develops the image (and the taunt) further with the lines (**26–8**), 'And Shylock (for his own part) knew the bird was flidge, and then it is the complexion of them all to leave the dam.' A fledgling will leave the nest when its wings have grown.
- Shylock then retorts with a pun (**27**), 'She is damned for it.' What is happening here? How does Shylock perform this line? He has lost his daughter and his jewels, one of which is a ring he had from his wife Leah (**line 111**). (Though we may reasonably assume that Leah was his wife, we don't *know* it.) He is being taunted by two particularly dislikeable characters, and yet he makes a pun part of his response. Is he joking with them? To declare that his daughter is damned would fit with the emotion of the scene, but to do so in the form of a pun as part of an extended word-play is another matter altogether.
- But then Salerio likens Shylock to the devil, and the emotional temperature starts to build.

After a few more exchanges between Salerio and Shylock on the subject of the difference between Shylock and Jessica, Shylock launches into one of his most famous speeches, which is in prose and not, in any strict form, a soliloquy. However, it demands a high pitch of emotion in the performance, and is also an intensely political speech (which curiously contains many ideas from Christian teaching, but this may be a case of Shakespeare using what is familiar and lacking an intimate knowledge of Judaic ethics). The task for the actor is to find a way by which he may project the emotion without losing the meaning.

One significant clue embedded in the language of this remarkable speech is that most of the sentences are in the form of questions. The listing of wrongs against him and his nation forms a taxonomy that allows the actor to build the pitch, but the fact that they end with a question shapes into coherence what could, otherwise, become a rant on stage. To ask to whom this speech is delivered could usefully open debate in the rehearsal room. Personally, I would favour a careful choreographing of the speech to allow a fluid movement that treats Salerio and Solanio as a surrogate audience juxtaposed to the actual audience. The last two lines (**65–6**) of this speech may carry dire warnings for a present-day audience, but this is a matter that must be left to the discretion of the reader and any future audience.

Salerio and Solanio are called away to Antonio's house, presumably to hear the news of his ships' failures. Tubal arrives when Shylock's anger is still driving the scene, but now his relationship with the other character on stage must change, and, I sense, his relationship with the audience must change with it. This is a dialogue between two old friends, albeit that Tubal brings more bad news relating to Jessica, and the audience's 'role' in this moment is metaphorically to step back and observe. Shylock must retreat from the audience to listen and to understand the full impact of what Tubal has to report, and to plan his revenge. We leave the scene, not at a high emotional level, but with Shylock again preparing for action.

Act III, scene ii (scene 14)

325 lines
Belmont

Plot objectives

As we are whisked away from the tension and the looming dark clouds in Venice, we return to what has hitherto formed the narrative focus of the play: the hoped-for romance between Portia and Bassanio. If the play is simply a romantic comedy then this scene should be its climax, but Shakespeare has created a far more complex narrative by sowing the seeds of disaster for Antonio and inviting our anticipation of the way this crisis will be resolved.

The scene is in two parts: the choosing of the correct casket by Bassanio, who thus wins Portia as his prize, together with the revelation of the Nerissa/Gratiano coupling; and the news that Antonio has been arrested, leading to Bassanio's imminent departure to attempt a rescue, which also means that the consummation of the marriage will be delayed until resolution has been achieved.

Setting

Given that this scene gives every reason for us to feel that a rite of passage is being performed, the presentation of the caskets requires something more than a scene representative of a marriage bargain being struck. If the winning of the Golden Fleece awarded wisdom to the winner, the choosing of the right casket requires wisdom and insight. Either Bassanio is given clues by Portia, or he does possess and demonstrate wisdom in choosing the lead casket.

Action, language and actors

The essential task in this scene is to establish the relationship between Portia and Bassanio. This is not an easy business. While we now know a fair amount about each character, they haven't yet met; at least they haven't met within the time span of the play, and that is what is of importance to us. Any other meeting they may have had outside the parameters of the play is a matter for conjecture and can only be of passing interest to us. So what will drive this scene is how the actors manage to work their way through the nuances of change as this relationship is presented to us.

The first point to note is how Portia seems to have undergone a subtle change in her behaviour. She may well have been 'aweary of this great world' when we first met her, but most of her actions and speeches would suggest that she is pretty determined and outspoken in her xenophobia. Now, however, she seems to have become unnerved by Bassanio's presence. Her opening speech (**lines 1–23**), framed in blank verse, as is most of the scene, signals to the audience the importance of the events, and is a delaying tactic expressive of her wish that she could find a way of teaching Bassanio how to choose the right casket. Clearly, she has fallen in love with Bassanio and her usual incisiveness and wit have forsaken her. Would we have expected Portia to become indecisive, as in the lines, 'One half of me is yours, the other half yours, – / Mine own I would say: but if mine then yours, / And so all yours; these naughty times . . .'. Clearly they do live in 'naughty' times and Belmont, in Portia's eyes, is an oasis that shines like a good deed in this naughty world. (For the correct quotation see Act V, **line 91**). Has the 'naughty world' of Venice come to Belmont in the shape of this young man? However we read the meaning in this speech, the actor playing Portia has to be able to turn on the proverbial sixpence in order to communicate Portia's present emotional state. She may be helped by the formality of the language. Is there a possibility that this is an act on Portia's part? In which case, the actor has an even more complicated task in appearing sincere while performing the rhetoric of uncertainty. Alternatively, we may argue that Portia's confessional ecstasy demands verse if it is to be captured.

In contrast to Portia's desire to delay the choice, Bassanio is eager to make the choice immediately so as to ease his uncertainty: 'Let me choose, / For as I am, I live upon the rack' (**lines 24–5**). There is a contorted passion in their word-play between **lines 24 and 39**, about which the actors must decide. Is the passion genuine? If so, the actors have to launch into it with little or no stage preparation. Or is it a rhetorical device that is performed within the fiction of the scene as much as it is performed to an audience? The language certainly is high-flown to an almost ludicrous extent.

As Bassanio approaches the caskets, a song is performed while he considers his choice. Many critics argue that the song, 'Tell me where is fancy bred . . .', contains clues as to which casket Bassanio should choose, and some have gone so far as to draw conclusions from the rhyming of *bred*, *head* and *nourished* (with the emphasis on the last syllable) with 'lead'. We may conjecture that the point of the song is to say that outward looks may deceive, and Bassanio takes up this theme in his first line: 'So may the outward shows be least themselves' (**line 72**). Has he heard a clue in the song? There may be nothing in any of these interpretations, and the song, as John Russell Brown suggests in the footnotes to our text, may be simply a device to remove the tedium of a 'third recital of the mottoes on the caskets'. Certainly, the performance of the song further delays the moment of choosing and thus builds dramatic tension.

Bassanio now has a very long speech to perform as he ponders on the choice before him. The speech is, for such a formal or even ritualistic moment, interestingly intimate and internalized. We have, it would seem, the whole of Belmont looking on as well as the audience, and Portia, we assume, is in a high state of tension. Yet, here is Bassanio musing on a number of philosophical points: 'damned error' is often explained away by citing scriptural text; the outward show of cowards may belie their inner failings, 'livers white as milk'. The whole speech is a discourse on the disparity between outward show and inner truth. The nature of the speech calls for introspection on the part of Bassanio and that can only be played at an intimate level. But where on the stage do we play this speech? One option on an open stage is to leave the household and the caskets up stage and bring Bassanio down stage amongst the audience, not to engage them directly as we might with a soliloquy, but to be alone among them.

The choice once made, the mood changes to celebration. By his choice Bassanio may 'come by note to give and to receive' (**line 140**). The inference is often taken that this speech ends (**line 148**) with a kiss, a simple enough matter on the present-day stage, but not so in the original context of production. Too often this factor is ignored, and yet, the way the language is formally constructed offers clues to a formalized moment of expression of love, rather than intimate physical contact. The sonnet spoken between Romeo and Juliet at their first meeting (*Romeo and Juliet*, Act I, scene v, lines 92–105) is a good example of formalized expressions of love.

Portia is still lacking in assurance, and her speech (**lines 149–74**) belies the wit we have heard and will experience in the future. At what level should the actor playing Portia pitch this apparent self-effacement?

With the arrival of Lorenzo, Jessica and Salerio from Venice the mood changes. Salerio reports that Antonio's maritime adventures have failed and he can no longer meet the terms of Shylock's bond. Shylock is determined to see that he has his pound of flesh. The news has a striking effect on Portia, whose demeanour changes from self-effacement in the presence of Bassanio to decisive action. With this change of mood must come a change in the dynamics of the stage action. Where there was stillness before, now the scene demands movement, which will re-focus the audience's attention to a gesturally dynamic moment as decisions are made.

As an afterthought, it does occur to me that Bassanio and Portia's 'courtship' in this scene is reminiscent of the courtship dance of various species of birds. The male bird often possesses florid plumage and displays it to the female, who, if impressed, acquiesces. Bassanio is the one who struts with his language, while Portia is, unusually, acquiescent; a small point, but one that might help us to embody the nature of the relationship throughout the courtship ritual in the choosing of the caskets.

Act III, scene iii (scene 15)

36 lines
Venice

Plot objectives

After the climax of the romantic comedy, we are given a short scene that, in its invocation of imminent brutality, shocks us back to Venice and reality. Antonio is ruined and faces a violent death.

Setting

This is one of those scenes where the action is in passing. On a proscenium stage, it may have taken place in front of the curtain on a short fore-stage, as we are to return to Belmont in only 36 lines and the curtain would need to be closed so that sets could be changed. On an open stage, with the intrinsic fluidity of that form of performance space, this would not present any problem.

Action, language and actors

In many ways this is a preparatory scene for the trial scene to come. It is in blank verse throughout, the iambic pentameter respected, which suggests that we keep a certain formality to the acting out of the confrontation between Shylock and Antonio when Shylock orders Antonio's arrest. The actors may take the scene in two ways. Depending on how we wish to present Shylock, we may see his anger as a way of lashing out at Antonio as the source of all his troubles:

from the past insults on the Rialto to Jessica's absconding with a Christian and his gold and jewels. On the other hand we may see this short, verbally violent scene as an indication of Shylock's real 'nature'; that it is not so much a case of the injured Jewish man, but more that his Jewishness is ultimately irrelevant because he is a bad man. Any rehearsal process should not wait until working on this scene before making such decisions, but in preliminary read-throughs by directors and actors this scene may, paradoxically, lead us backwards to decisions to be made prior to the start of rehearsals.

There is an interesting moment of which we should take careful note. **Lines 19–24** are spoken by Antonio to Solanio, after Shylock has left the stage, on, 'I'll have no speaking, I will have my bond' (**line 17**). Antonio's short speech suggests that Shylock is an irredeemable man who seeks vengeance against Antonio because Antonio has 'oft deliver'd from his forfeitures / Many that have at times made moan to me, / Therefore he hates me'. Do we, from this information, have more sympathy for Antonio? We only have Antonio's word for it, whereas Shylock's accusations of mistreatment by Antonio are supported by Antonio's not only agreeing that he has 'spat upon his Jewish gaberdine', but saying that he would do it again.

These short scenes reveal much information that must become central to our portrayal of the relationship between these two men.

Act III, scene iv (scene 16)

84 lines
Belmont

Plot objectives

Meanwhile, back in Belmont, Bassanio and Gratiano having already left for Venice on their mission of mercy; Lorenzo praises Antonio to Portia. Portia, in her turn, decides that Antonio must be held in the same esteem as her lord and husband. (Do we really believe this?) Unbeknown to anyone, she has already in mind her plan to intervene in the trial back in Venice. Is this because she is so convinced by the idea that Antonio is as worthy as her husband that she must add every weight to the effort to save him? Or may there be other reasons? She is a woman of great wit (in its proper sense, meaning intelligence) and may see that simply throwing money at it may not solve the problem. Does this emphasize an ideological distinction between the values of the distinct worlds of Venice and Belmont? Or is Portia a mistress of pragmatism?

She bestows the husbandry of her estate on Lorenzo (curious, as she hardly knows him) and declares that both she and Nerissa will live in a state of celibacy and contemplation in a nearby monastery until their husbands return.

Once they are alone with Balthazar (why does she choose that name for her disguised self?), she gives him his instructions and reveals the plan to Nerissa. The scene ends with their surprise departure for Venice imminent.

Setting

Simply Belmont. The movement between this scene and Act III, scene ii would suggest that we need to create the effect that Portia has just seen Bassanio off on his journey and has come back into one of the public rooms of her house with her purpose fully formed. The caskets would not be present as they no longer serve any purpose, unless the design of the production deems them to be an ever-present symbol (one may stretch this image to their looming presence in Venetian scenes if pictorial scenography is to move beyond the literal in its imagery), in which case their disappearance by this scene would carry significance in our visual reading of the play's narrative.

Action, language and actors

The whole scene focuses on Portia. Whereas in earlier scenes we have seen enough to convince us that this woman is a force to be reckoned with, the performance of this scene has required her to act in a relatively passive manner; we have read in the previous scenes her reactions to events, and now we see her taking charge. The actor playing Portia must be prepared for this change in gear.

In the first part of the scene (**lines 1–44**) nearly all of her words are directed to Lorenzo and only two lines (**lines 43–4**) are to Jessica. This could mean everything and nothing. Does she disregard Jessica because she is Jewish, or is her attention focused on Lorenzo as a male and someone to whom Belmont might be entrusted. There is nothing in **lines 43 and 44** to suggest anything other than polite regard towards Jessica.

With Lorenzo and Jessica off stage, Portia may turn her energies towards her plan. In doing so there are several references that should be of interest to the actor in developing Portia's role in the scheme of things. In **lines 60–78** Portia gives an astute and witty account of the behaviour typical of young men that is strikingly similar to Rosalind's speech of liberation (Act I, scene iii, lines 113–21) in *As You Like It*. Moreover, she also reveals another aspect of her humour of which we should take serious note. In **lines 61–2 and 79–80** Portia makes sexually explicit jokes to Nerissa that, in essence, focus on male genitalia or the lack of them. These references are followed, in due course, by the sexual nature of the trick of the rings, which represent female genitalia. Remembering that Portia and Nerissa would have been played by boy actors in the original context, is there some element that should be noted by a female actor playing the role today? The information that may be gleaned from the intrinsic gender ambiguity in *As You Like It* may be of use in working this transition from Portia and Nerissa to the lawyer Balthazar and 'his' clerk.

Act III, scene v (scene 17)

85 lines
Belmont

Plot objectives

This is a curious short scene (one of a number) between Launcelot, Jessica and Lorenzo, which could be read in many ways, one of which is deeply anti-semitic. On the Elizabethan stage the scene may well have been run straight on from the previous scene without any clear break between the two. One purpose of this scene may have been to try to assimilate Lorenzo and Jessica, who hitherto have existed on the edge of events, into the rapid narrative developments. Another reason for this scene's presence may simply be that it gives Portia and Nerissa an opportunity to change costumes into Balthazar (the lawyer, not the servant) and his boy clerk, for the next scene.

Nothing happens except the exchange between the increasingly unfunny Launcelot and Jessica regarding the notion that, because she is a Jew, she is automatically damned. We may wish to note that certain of the more extreme forms of Protestantism taught that only a percentage of people were born to be saved, and that, no matter what you did in life, the outcome was predestined. Jessica counters Launcelot with the fact that she has become a Christian by her marriage to Lorenzo (citing St Paul – 1 Corinthians, 7, 14: 'The unbelieving wife is sanctified by the husband'). This exchange descends into banter with the suggestion that an increase in Christians will raise the price of pork (the eating of pork being forbidden to Jews). This level of low mercantile humour is a curiosity compounded by Lorenzo's revelation that Launcelot has impregnated a black servant of Portia's household (**lines 34–6**). Launcelot's retort is in the form of a predictable pun on the words 'Moor' and 'more'. The final exchange is between Lorenzo and Jessica, during which the lovers discuss Portia's virtues and Lorenzo parade's his own! This really does seem to be a 'filler' scene.

Setting

If, as we suspect, this scene is really a part of the previous one, then the setting will simply remain the same.

Action, language and actors

The scene is in two distinct parts in terms of both language and subject: the first is the exchange between Launcelot and Jessica, which brings Lorenzo into the matter, and is written in prose; the second is the discussion of Portia's (and Lorenzo's) virtues, and is in blank verse with a consistent measure of ten syllables to the line. The message to the actors is that we require quite different modes of delivery in the two parts of the scene.

What kind of relationship exists between Launcelot and Jessica? The evidence from earlier scenes suggests that they have a close and intimate, but innocent, relationship. Perhaps he has been a sympathetic companion in the loneliness that seems to have permeated her father's house. If their relationship is founded on positive values the dialogue of this scene suggests friendly banter. However, the prejudice at the root of the humour, whether it be anti-Semitic, or dismissive of the black servant whom Launcelot has 'lanced', while it may have been acceptable to an audience in past times, has discomforting resonances today. The scene could be acted as a kind of stand-up, knock-for-knock punning routine, which would offer, by its overt brutality, both an opportunity to 'frame' the offensive material in a discourse akin to *Verfremdung*, and a chance for Jessica to establish her presence. Otherwise, we may take the pathway offered by the anti-Semitism to lay the groundwork for Jessica's alienation at the end of the play, when the full force of Shylock's punishment is revealed.

The relative formality of the second part of the scene between the two lovers, Lorenzo and Jessica, is more difficult, not least because the actors must contend with the sudden change from prose to verse. Launcelot exits in prose at **lines 58–9**, and immediately Lorenzo launches into verse with his discourse on the Fool's departure and his seeking Jessica's impression of Portia. Lorenzo's steering of the dialogue towards self-praise could be left as a blatant example of the ludicrous and vainglorious if it were not for the tenor of Jessica's response in the final few lines (**79–85**). There is much here for the actor playing Jessica to think about. There can be no doubt that she introduces levels of complexity to the play's closure.

ACT IV

Act IV, scene i (scene 18)

453 lines
Venice

Plot objectives

If there was ever a scene that justified placing the initial impetus in the hands of the actors, this is it. The formality suggested by a court-room scene in whatever place or period is undermined by the manner in which formal rhetoric moves to rhetorical passion, and even threatens to turn to mob chaos. To allow actors to play with this scene before any kind of staging decisions are introduced will give a vitality that, otherwise, could easily be missed. (As an aside we may note that some productions bring Tubal on stage as a silent, and often condemnatory, witness to Shylock's determination to bring about *Antonio's downfall.*)

With the romantic plot having had its climax delayed we now reach the reason for the hiatus. The trial scene brings the Venetian part of the plot to its climax, and the particular plot objective of this scene is to determine the outcome of the bond, and the enmity between Shylock and Antonio, one way or another.

This scene, however, also brings the two separate worlds of Venice and Belmont together in ways that seem further to subvert the position of the men, and reinforce Portia's wit and wile. Venice, it may be argued, is already a world divided between the Christians and the Jews. It is of no matter what the accuracy of these tensions is historically, as it is this fictional Venice that demands our scrutiny. While historiography is one of our vital research tools, any results of that research can do no more than temper, or contextually frame, our close reading of the text. For example, it is fairly clear that the Duke is the Doge of Venice and that the Doge, certainly by the time of the sixteenth century, was unlikely to preside over cases of civil law, even one that was likely to result in a form of judicial murder; his place would have been supplied by three Counsellors. But does it ultimately matter? The text asks for the Duke. Moreover, it is rarely remembered that Portia actually acts as a judge rather than as an advocate and, therefore, should really be placed on a judgment seat beneath the Duke's throne. If we followed this line of thinking we would end up with a static scene that missed the opportunity for the legal dance that occurs between Portia and Shylock.

It is difficult to say who emerges from the trial scene with any honour, and, whichever way we may construct meanings from the scene, ambiguity of values seems to be the only constant in the collision of the three worlds of the play.

At one level, we may argue that the clear plot objective of this scene is already established from the beginning of the play, and that this objective is to secure the downfall of the Jew Shylock. This is, of course, one of the problems we have nowadays with the play. During the first part of the scene, **lines 1–118**, the Venetian Christian men are set on a course of, at the most depressing reading, Jew baiting. Even the Duke's seeming dilemma and ineffectual pleading with Shylock is but a precursor to Bassanio's impotent gesture of throwing money at the problem, and Gratiano's vile invective against Shylock. Shylock's responses will need careful analysis when we come to consider how the actor approaches their delivery, and how they sit against the speeches of the Duke, Bassanio, and Gratiano.

The *imminent* entry of Portia and Nerissa signals a change of key. The presence of Balthazar/Portia may be seen as a threat in Shylock's eyes, and a glimmer of hope for Antonio's cause. In the end the whole outcome depends upon definitions and, as this is a civil court of law (curious in itself as the outcome may involve 'judicial' murder), it would seem appropriate that, in law as in theatrical performance, everything hangs on the use of language – at least on the part of the Christian alliance between Venice and Belmont. In opposition, Shylock's case is based upon the spirit of the law/bond. Portia commences her work as a lawyer, not with a legal argument, but with a poetic plea for mercy. When this fails, she then exercises what really does appear to be legal trickery in the atomization (figuratively and literally) of the letter of the law.

The ensuing debate also sets the scene for Portia's testing of her husband's fidelity (**lines 421–5**) after Bassanio has previously declared his willingness to sacrifice his wife for Antonio's deliverance (**lines 278–85**), with Gratiano aping Bassanio's declared willingness to sacrifice his wife, and eliciting a similar response from Nerissa.

Setting

This is one scene where the setting, though not necessarily the set design, is of paramount importance. Whatever the physical shape of the performance space, where we place people and how we move them in relation to each other as the scene builds is crucial to the scene's meaning.

Even if a form of pictorial staging is the chosen approach, the fundamental questions we need to ask regarding the presentation of the trial are the same as those for more flexible forms of staging. Irrespective of the precise architecture of our imagined Venetian court of civil law, we must translate certain hierarchies of social position into physical positions on the stage, as well as recording the shifting socio/personal relationships of the characters as the narrative of the scene develops, prompting often subtle changes of position. We may, for example, observe that the developing relationship between Shylock and Portia in this scene is a kind of dance performed through the complicated thickets of poetic pleas for mercy and then becoming a more brutal choreography of legal language. In order to gain a sense of this kind of patterning, we need to work through the stages of the scene's development and ask questions apposite to any one moment.

For the first fifteen lines, Shylock is not on the stage. We may assume that the 'setting', as we may now call it, is fairly straightforward. Although the Duke of Venice has had no previous significance in this story, and indeed has little significance in the action of this scene (his is one of those difficult high-authority roles to play, with precious little offered in terms of character significance), he only has six lines in which to establish his stage and narrative significance before Shylock makes his entrance.

One of those interesting contradictions between the dramatic performance and the 'realities' of the fictional world is to be found in the moment Shylock is made to wait outside the courtroom. It is the authority of the Duke that dictates that the play's major antagonist be kept waiting outside. But theatrically it raises Shylock's status as it only serves to intensify the audience's suspense and expectation. The social hierarchy of the fictional world may reduce Shylock, but the theatrical device paradoxically raises his stage status.

In these **first 15 lines**, a fairly predictable outcome of the practicalities of stagecraft is that we assume that the Duke is positioned on the stage in such a way that he commands attention. Does he stand 'upstage centre'? Does he sit on some kind of raised dais? Movement is not suggested by either his social function, or his language; unless, of course, we wish to challenge the norms of expectation by some form of radical staging. The received notion of the trial's social hierarchies may be highlighted by either framing or subverting them.

We await Shylock's entrance. How does he enter? The Duke's first lines indicate that there is a crowd: 'Make room, and let him stand before our face.' If the Duke is still, what of everyone else? Visually, Shylock needs to be separated from the general crowd, but what is the nature of this crowd? The behaviour of some people, in particular Gratiano, would suggest that it is more like a mob. The 'crowd' only demands Antonio, Bassanio, Gratiano and Salerio as speaking roles, but could be as big, or as small, as theatrical economies may permit.

The Duke and Shylock have their two big set pieces, **lines 16–34 and lines 35–62** respectively. Do we assume that, in terms of setting, these are fairly static pieces of rhetoric? Is there another way by which the moment may be brought to life on the stage?

From **lines 63 to 142** the previous formality of the setting breaks down into a brawl between Shylock and, mainly, Bassanio, with Gratiano railing against Shylock to no particular purpose. We need to consider carefully the level to which we wish the stage positions to break away from any preconceived norm of a trial setting. It could be reduced to people sitting around a table (this was the chosen mode in the Miller/Olivier production described in Chapter 3), or a contrived mêlée could break out. There is a brief hiatus at **lines 119–20** on Nerissa's entrance, announcing the imminent arrival of Portia/ Balthazar. This must be noticed as the people in the audience need to have the opportunity to build their expectation of the other main character's arrival. **Line 146** brings all stage movement to a halt with the reading of the letter from Bellario.

From **line 165 to line 403** the pace and the setting changes as Portia, effectively and perhaps literally, takes stage centre. Portia and Shylock now debate the issue (which we will examine in detail in the next section). Physically, they both need stage space, and, apart from the odd interjection from Bassanio and Gratiano, the setting is for a legal debate.

The final section (**lines 404–53**) does not offer any significant problems regarding the setting of the scene. The Duke, his train, and Shylock have gone, leaving the characters from the romantic plot alone on stage, apart from the new element in that narrative, Antonio.

Action, language and actors

Given the pre-eminence of Shylock and Portia in this scene – Antonio, as ever, does not seem to be actively engaged despite what is about to happen to him, and Bassanio and Gratiano rail ineffectively – we need to step back for a moment in order that we might consider (and reconsider) our perceptions of Shylock and Portia. To do so is a necessary reassessment as this is the first time the two are on stage together and we will need to allow the actors to gain the measure of each other. (In fact, if our rehearsal process follows conventional lines as it might, say, with the RSC, the actors playing Shylock and Portia will not have even worked together until they reach this point in the schedule. Of course, this need not be our template for rehearsal methods.)

Where do we place Shylock racially and culturally? Our decision here may determine the nature of his performance under duress in the trial. We tread on dangerous ground, but we should be giving thought to vocal mannerisms and gestural qualities that speak of the character's origin but without reinforcing cultural or racial stereotypes, unless we do so with a particular purpose in mind. We might be led into assuming that Shylock is an assimilated Jew from the evidence of Portia's line just after her entrance, 'Which is the merchant here? And which the Jew?' (**line 170**). Is this question caused by the fact that all present are dressed and behaving in the same manner? The actor Edwin Booth's response is noted in the New Variorum edition (edited by H. H. Furness in 1888): 'After a look of surprise, he replies doggedly' that his name is Shylock (see note 184). What may this tell us about the presentation of Shylock? Or is something else happening at this moment? Is it a tactic employed by Portia for reasons best known to herself? Whichever way we read that moment, it is important that the actor playing Portia knows what she means, as it may set the mode for playing Portia in the whole of this scene.

Shylock, curiously for someone who has, throughout the play, demonstrated his tendency to place monetary value above all, now returns to the bond, which demands not money, or even property, but a human body, or at least a part of it. A perverse circle has been turned and is exposed by the trial. The valuing of people for their humanity has been displaced by their valuation as financial commodities: Antonio for his ability to stand as surety for a loan; Portia as represented by the caskets. But the human body, so far removed from humanity in this play, has now achieved the power to fuel and satiate human emotions; it has become reunited with 'humanity', but in a most grotesque version.

Shylock and the actor playing him are in a most difficult position. If he has been presented until now with a degree of sympathy, how do we sustain that interpretation through the trial? If he has been presented as a villain throughout, we will need to handle with care the Venetians' treatment of him at the end of the trial. For it is only by playing them sympathetically, that the idea of the 'villain' brought to a just end will work dramatically. The simple lesson we should take note of here is to play our reading of the play consistently, and not to be seduced into inconsistency by the many complex twists and turns of this scene. Terry Eagleton suggests that Shylock has never expected to win the case. He argues that, as the despised outsider, Shylock is curious to see what the outcome of his confronting the Venetian ruling class will be, and what device they will manufacture to allow Antonio to escape. Eagleton goes on to wonder if, in the playing of this scene, Shylock performs as much to the audience as to the other characters, 'throwing them [*the audience*] a knowing wink when Portia produces her knockdown argument' (Eagleton, 1986, pp. 37–8).

Our first meeting with Portia is as we catch her bemoaning her world-weariness in mid-conversation with Nerissa, and not much that happens in the ensuing scenes prepares us for the *régisseur* who controls affairs from the end of Act III, scene iv, to the end of the play. Admittedly, there are flashes of wit and even evidence of a sharp tongue before this point, but, in contrast to her seeming submissiveness in the moment after Bassanio has chosen the right casket, Portia now emerges as decisive and, it would seem, also a graduate in law. The transition is not immediate and Shakespeare does allow the actor and us some breathing space for the 'new' Portia to emerge, with Act III, scene iv, providing the transition in which the actor is able to adopt this new aspect of Portia's character.

The entrances of both Shylock and Portia are theatrically and dramatically important. Shylock's entrance has been dealt with and so, in one sense, has Portia's. At the risk of labouring the point, the line 'Which is the merchant here? And which the Jew?' (**line 170**) creates a moment of unexpected theatrical hiatus in which all the other characters, including Shylock, are thrown slightly off balance. Isn't it obvious who the Jew is to the Venetian eye? This is the 'new' Portia's real entrance, one which allows her to gain dramatic and visual space in the performance as the other characters momentarily look from one to the other in slight confusion, while the audience wonders who will be the first to speak. It may be a tiny moment in the grand narrative of the play, but it is one that affords Portia authority and the actor a commanding stage position. Where the actor stands for this moment is open to debate and will, to an extent, depend on our chosen performance space. It is a moment that calls out for the actor and the director to take a risk.

Now, if we move to examine the scene closely, we see that **lines 16–62** are taken up by a fairly formal exchange between the Duke and Shylock. The Duke's speech presages Portia's famous 'mercy' speech, but seems to be driven by confusion. The Venetian court does not seem to know what to do with Shylock and so resorts to a plea of mercy on behalf of Antonio, one of their own.

The Duke's speech is closer to rhetorical stasis than it is to action. Shylock's reply is equally static in terms of stage action, but his refusal to countenance mercy, or to give any reason why, 'But to say that it is my humour' (**line 43**), followed by his quite extraordinary images, does suggest more and more that he is intrigued to see how far he can push this court of law. If Shylock is to play this scene with a knowing wink to the audience (the kind of conspiracy in which an actor may engage with the audience, particularly in soliloquies), this is where it starts. On the final line (**62**) ' – are you answered?' may take the form of a stage gesture that turns from the Duke and Bassanio to the audience. **Lines 63–9** take us from the formality of the Duke's plea for mercy and the ambiguity of Shylock's reply to a quick-fire exchange with Bassanio that prepares the ground for later blasts of hatred expressed by all parties.

The kind of conspiracy between actor/character and audience that may be possible for Shylock does not come as easily to him as it does to other major protagonists. Richard III enters immediately into a knowing conspiracy with the audience (so naughtiness, in the sixteenth-century sense of the word, is not an impediment), and Hamlet is more often in contact with the audience than with any other persons in the play. If Shylock is an uncertain conspirator, it may be because he is self-alienating as well as alienated by the 'naughty' society in which he lives. He lacks, we might say, the naughty charm of Richard III.

Antonio has given up! His reactions to the trial mirror the melancholy with which he greets us in the first lines of the play. While Bassanio bargains for his life with ducats, Antonio becomes more and more passive. The actor has a difficult task throughout the play: Antonio is the eponymous figure in the play, but the least effective figure in the play's progress. The actor must establish Antonio's presence, while doing little to drive forward the narrative. While Antonio's passivity is encapsulated in **lines 70–83**, the audience is given breathing space before Shylock is stung into reaction by the Duke's line 'How shalt thou hope for mercy rend'ring none?' (**88**).

The comparative moderation of Antonio's speech and Bassanio's attempts to buy his freedom allow Shylock's outburst to take full effect (**lines 89–103**). It is as if years of pent-up alienation, insult and bigotry finally find their outlet in an onslaught on Venetian Christian hypocrisy. It is Shylock's last chance to say something that rises above the immediate demands of the scene's narrative before Portia's ever-so-subtly metaphorical legal knife starts to take effect, initially under the guise of the plea for mercy, but with the sting in the tail that begins with, 'Tarry a little, there is something else' (**line 301**). Shylock's speech ends with a question, 'I stand for judgement, – answer, shall I have it?' (**line 104**). His question will be answered, and in the harshest of tones.

The flow of the scene is now broken by Nerissa's entrance, and while the Duke reads Bellario's letter of introduction to Balthazar/Portia, a near riot breaks out in the verbally violent exchange between Shylock and Gratiano (**lines 121–42**). (Gratiano uses the word 'inexecrable', which seems to exist nowhere else in English. While it has no defined meaning, it speaks volumes.) The riot that has almost broken out suggests that any formalizing of stage movement up until now should be broken up so that action mirrors language. This will then allow the Duke's interjection, 'This letter from Bellario doth commend . . .' (**line 143**) (has the Duke not noticed the near riot going on around him?), to signal the start of a more ordered focus to the scene's narrative. In reading the letter out loud, the Duke furnishes us, the audience, as well as the characters in the scene, with the necessary information by which we may accept the convention of Portia arriving dressed as a man. Practice in the theatre has demonstrated, time and time again, that an audience will accept the most unlikely instances in a plot, as long as the stage convention is clearly established for all to see.

Portia takes command of the scene and the stage, as we have already seen, with the line 'Which is the merchant here? And which the Jew?' The long dance between Shylock and Portia now begins.

The actor playing Portia now has one of those fiendishly difficult moments in the modern performance of Shakespeare's plays, particularly in the context of 'western' theatre. She has to perform a speech knowing that a good part of the audience have not only been waiting for this moment, but will be mouthing it silently with her. 'The quality of mercy is not strain'd' (**line 180**), apart from being a staggeringly beautiful evocation of mercy, ranks alongside Hamlet's 'To be or not to be' as a soliloquy that is at least semi-known by nearly everyone in the English-speaking world. While Portia's speech follows on from the Duke's plea for mercy, it is also the start of Portia's move to tighten the screws on Shylock, a last-ditch attempt – more eloquent than the Duke's – to appeal to Shylock's better nature.

The actor's task from now on is not easy. Remember, she has to appear as the commander of the proceedings, in contrast to her earlier appearances, and now she has to play one game while, surely, plotting another. From **line 214 through to line 301**, she follows the letter of the law whilst appearing to favour Shylock's legal case (if not

Shylock himself), without abandoning her plea to temper legal right with mercy. But the final twist of her metaphorical knife, just before Shylock's literal knife touches Antonio's bosom, cannot simply be a spur-of-the-moment flash of insight. Or can it? Whichever path the actor chooses – a genuine plea for mercy and, when that fails, a sudden realization that there is a flaw in the bond to be exploited, or a calculated plot to corner Shylock and destroy him – the performing of Portia will require subtly different nuances.

The two actors, if their legal 'dance' is to achieve consistency and to hold the audience's focus, will have to work closely together; this is their one and only chance, in the whole play, to achieve this level of interaction. By achieving this complex interaction with clarity, they may just be able to give us a glimpse of the social tragedy lurking in the shadows of a romantic comedy. Such action on stage would make problematic the easy categorizing of Shakespeare's play into any clearly defined genre, and offer a more subtle insight into human relationships as depicted through drama.

There is one moment of vital interaction between Portia and Bassanio (and to a lesser extent Nerissa and Gratiano) to which we need to give some attention, as it bears significantly on their respective relationships and on events to come in the curiously separate 'Scene 20' (or, as for many actors who have played Shylock, the gratuitous Act V) when we return to the romantic comedy. Between **lines 278 and 290** (and possibly including Antonio's speech in the preceding **lines 260–77**, and Shylock's following **lines 291–4**) there is a pointed exchange between Portia/Bassanio and Nerissa/Gratiano, which is commented on by Shylock, the staging of which needs careful consideration.

The exchange starts with **lines 260–83** and reveals an intimacy between Antonio and Bassanio that, if it does not necessarily imply sexual love, certainly goes beyond that of mere friendship. Antonio's words elicit a response from Bassanio that, however temporarily, threatens the status of his newly won wife. Bassanio's balancing of relationships is clumsy, perhaps, but the primary challenge to the actors here is to achieve an inset of intimacy in the crowded courtroom. Of course, as was demonstrated skilfully and pointedly by Trevor Nunn in the television adaptation of his stage production, film and video may achieve this by selective camera shots. There is a moment in Nunn's production when the shot is framed by Bassanio (screen right), standing and leaning towards the seated Antonio (screen left). This framing of the screen in its turn created for the viewer a glimpse of Portia's pointed reaction (**lines 284–5**) as she turned from shuffling papers on a table to respond both visually and verbally to Bassanio's readiness to 'lose all, ay sacrifice them all / Here to this devil, to deliver you' (**lines 282–3**). How do we achieve this 'tight-focus' intimacy on our various forms of stage? Shylock effectively ends the exchange with a comment, which must be delivered to the audience '[*Aside*] These be the Christian husbands!' This is not a question to be answered at this juncture; its value is in the asking.

There are two more points of action to ponder before we leave this scene: first, the various reactions to Shylock's downfall; secondly, the manner in which Portia maintains control of events and relationships through the stage business of the rings.

As we have noticed with, for example, the scene between Portia and Morocco, unspoken reactions can speak as loudly as words. Of course Shylock may rail against Venetian 'justice', he may disintegrate before our very eyes, or he may (in the fashion of Laurence Olivier) deliver a heart-rending cry off-stage. But, whatever way we decide Shylock should react to what is meted out to him (and we should take note of his **line 392**, 'I am not well, send the deed after me'), the power of the moments before his departure lives also in how Portia and the Venetians react to what has been done.

From **line 343** (Portia's second 'Tarry Jew') through to his exit on **line 394**, the words are concerned with outlining what the state of Venice and the court allows by way of punishment for Shylock, as an alien (**line 345**). These exchanges, apart from the predictable outbursts from Gratiano (**lines 360–3 and 375**), can be handled in a business-like legal manner. Venice has done its job with cool efficiency and there is no noticeable sense that anything is amiss; quite the contrary, everything has turned out well. Alternatively, a collective animosity could seep through the legalistic tones of the speeches to the point of Shylock's departure. How Shylock then finishes the scene and makes his exit will provide the opportunity for the full impact of the trial's outcome to be embodied in the

Venetians' reaction to what has been done. There may well be general indifference to his fate, or it may be that a collective guilt is expressed silently.

Once the aftershock of Shylock's departure has begun to subside, Portia/Balthazar switches our attention to the rings. This is an extra-ordinary exercise of control – masterful insistence that life must go on, however bleak the context. The boldness of Shakespeare's writing is supremely illustrated in this dramaturgical *volte-face*. Is this the same submissive Portia we observed after Bassanio had made his correct choice of the caskets? The actor playing Portia, having taken control of the 'tragic' trial, now has the power to steer the play towards comedy. We prepare for the imminent return to Belmont, the home of comedy.

Act IV, scene ii (scene 19)

19 lines
Venice

Plot objectives

In these 19 lines, the only objective is to give time to reset Belmont (if pictorial staging is the chosen mode), or to allow Gratiano the moment in which to give Portia Bassanio's ring and for Nerissa to gull Gratiano out of his ring as they proceed to Shylock's house. The audience senses Bassanio and Gratiano's discomfort over the loss of the rings and looks ahead to Portia's response.

Setting

As this scene is so short, we may assume that it is one of those moments in a proscenium theatre that would be performed in front of the curtain while Belmont is reset. However, on the Elizabethan stage this is a busy 'door' scene, which begins with Gratiano following Nerissa through one door, and ends with Gratiano's perplexity as Nerissa leaves through the other door. All he can do is retrace his steps.

Action, language and actors

In one sense this cannot really count as a scene. Portia and Nerissa have left the stage only nine lines before and we may imagine that they take a quick tour through the Tiring House, or across backstage, in order that they may be seen to enter through another door or stage entrance. The purpose of the action is to ensure that the ring plot is set and that we are embarked on the return to comedy, unlikely as that prospect might seem after the events of the previous 453 lines. The associated requirement is that the actors ensure that the scene is delivered crisply and clearly in order that the ring plot is set up clearly. The audience will otherwise, as with any 'comic intrigue' episode, miss the detail.

ACT V (SCENE 20)

307 lines
Belmont

Plot objectives

This final scene really should not be there if we agree with many lawgivers on dramatic construction. There is, they might claim, a fault in Shakespeare's composition in allowing a weak scene to finish a play after a strong scene in which the play's serious business is concluded. But should we agree? And when did Shakespeare ever cling to the strict laws of composition or genre?

If members of the audience are preparing to gather their belongings for a quick exit from the theatre after Shylock leaves the stage, the last lines of Act IV, scene i, along with the 'interlude' of scene ii, disrupt that early departure by introducing another plot: the trick of the rings. We should also remember that clear-cut divisions between concepts of dramatic genre such as tragedy and comedy, histories and romances, are essentially a matter of the editorial desire to tidy up the Shakespearean canon. *The Merchant of Venice* is not the only play by Shakespeare to confuse the critical impulse to categorize.

Even so, the leap from the shadow of tragedy back to romantic comedy via Act IV, scene ii, is a difficult adjustment for an audience, as well as for the performers to achieve, and is made especially so when none of the romantic characters has done much to deserve our affection. Perhaps it is best for all concerned that we put aside any attempts to resolve issues of dramatic structure according to pre-set rules. In doing so, we may understand that Shakespeare possessed an astute understanding of the evidence of experience that tells us that human actions, even when distilled into dramatic form, do not work as neatly as some dramatic theories would have us believe. There is a temptation, which I will resist only to the extent that I will not make an issue out of it, to relate Shakespeare's understanding that life is fragmented, in an unnervingly similar way, to the experiences articulated through the art of the modernist twentieth century. This is not a retrospective plea in support for Shakespeare the universal genius, reaching through 400 years. It is more a recognition of the way that I find Shakespeare possesses an ability to dislocate my expectations of his purpose.

There are two main parts to the scene and both are concerned with the play's romantic conclusion. First of all we have this disturbingly beautiful sub-scene between Lorenzo and Jessica, the purpose of which may be to allow the actors their moment, or perhaps, at last, to bring these two marginal characters into the foreground. They are, after all, bound inextricably to Shylock's future by the will of the court and of Antonio. The second objective is to bring the lovers to resolution once more, back at Belmont the beautiful hill, and, of course, to resolve the trick of the rings before they all depart to the delayed consummation of their marriages.

However, even at this point of romantic resolution, there are two elements that can only be teased out of the play text by visual stage action. There are no words to indicate how we leave Antonio and Jessica, only the sense that finding a place for them in this new world may not be all that easy.

What kind of life is there for Antonio now that his 'love' Bassanio is married? Will he sink deeper into melancholia? It is not our business to delve into the past and future lives of the characters. They live only in the moment of the play. But we do, as theatre makers, need to know what the actor playing Antonio is doing on stage in the last few moments of the play. Can he really be following the lovers in to the house, knowing they can't wait to leap into bed with each other? How is Jessica to react to the news of what has been done to her father? How is she to fit into this Christian world, now being of it and yet not of it? And if we look at Portia's **lines 288–9**, we may note that it is to Lorenzo that she gives the 'good comforts' that he is to gain Shylock's wealth after his death. I have a strong sense that all may not be resolved for Jessica and Antonio. It is not uncommon for someone to be left out of the general happiness at the end of one of Shakespeare's comedies, but usually it is someone, such as Malvolio, who we may argue has brought the exclusion upon himself. Here it is the Merchant of the play's title, Antonio, and Jessica, who seems to be one of the more likeable characters, unless she be blamed for being Jewish and having stolen her father's jewels – but isn't that what the Venetians have just done?.

Setting

Whatever the chosen form of performance space, this final scene of the play demands particular attention to the way in which time and place are indicated. The place, of course, is Belmont, and the time moves from night to dawn. How we indicate these settings today depends very much on the style of staging, as we may move through the possible spectrum from a full pictorial setting to a minimalist setting in which, apart from the imagery offered by the language, stage lighting could well fulfil all needs of time and location. Martin Banham, in his essay ' *The Merchant of Venice* and the Implicit Stage Direction', is referring to the original context of staging in the Elizabethan playhouse, and offers an intriguing breakdown of action and setting through the images embedded in the language (Banham, 1991). Thus we know that it is the afternoon in the theatre where the play is being performed, but we are given plenty of information from which to deduce the notion that the early action between Lorenzo and Jessica is taking place by moonlight. Moreover, because the scene is played between two male actors, it is the language that must convey their lovemaking, and not physical contact.

As the scene proceeds with Portia and Nerissa nearing this oasis in a naughty world, 'How far that candle throws his beams! / So shines a good deed in a naughty world. / When the moon shone we did not see the candle' (**lines 89–92**), we realize that the candle's beam is not so strong as it was because dawn is breaking. (In passing, it is worth noting that the term 'naughty' carried a much stronger resonance than it does today. For 'naughty' today read 'wicked'.)

Again, Banham draws our attention to a metatheatrical quality to this scene, of the type that we find in so many of Shakespeare's plays when the words on the page draw attention to the physical aspects of the theatre in which the scene is being played and employ them as a part of the action of the scene. Drawing on **lines 54–65** in Lorenzo's speech, 'How sweet the moonlight sleeps upon this bank! ...', Banham points out that Lorenzo invites Jessica to sit and then draws her attention to the way 'the floor of heaven / is thick inlaid with patens of bright gold' (**lines 58–9**), which are most likely to be the images painted on the cloth suspended above the stage in the public playhouse and known in the theatre as 'the heavens'. This example does not really relate in any direct sense to the later pictorial scenography of the nineteenth and twentieth centuries, as the 'heavens', as far as we know, were more or less permanent features of the playhouse and not directly related, in a pictorial, scenographic sense, to *The Merchant of Venice*, or any other play. It is on these grounds that the reference in Lorenzo's speech is metatheatrical and emblematic, rather than illusory. The reference draws attention to the theatre, rather than creating an illusion of sitting under the stars at Belmont.

We do not enter the house in Belmont, as most of the characters do eventually, so we must assume that the scene takes place in the garden where we are to remain with Lorenzo and Jessica, awaiting each arrival from Venice. Indeed, this is where we the audience are left (perhaps with Antonio and Jessica) when Portia, Bassanio, Nerissa and Gratiano depart indoors for the consummation of their marriages.

Action, language and actors

A Grove or Green Place before Portia's House is the setting for the action to begin. The last moments we experienced saw the delivery of the papers Shylock is to be forced to sign and the setting up of the trick of the rings. The last moments of the trial scene, and all the interlude of the scene that follows it, demand crisp business-like action on stage. Now – and in the flick of an eye, if we are working on an open stage – we are transported into a love scene, the very quality of which requires the audience, led by the actors playing Lorenzo and Jessica, to accept the quiet, gently flirtatious relationship that is being acted out between **lines 1 and 24**. A gentle rhythm is set by the repetition of, 'In such a night . . .' at the start of each speech, and while the mood thus created is of the two lovers playing an intimate word game on the theme of classical lovers, the choice of subject matter is to do with tragedy and betrayal: Troilus and Cressida; Pyramus and Thisbe (not Bottom's version in *A Midsummer Night's Dream*, we assume!); Dido and Aeneas; and Medea and Jason. A curious choice of subject matter, without doubt, in the case of the first three, but the fourth is a little more ambiguous as no direct reference is made to Jason at this point in the play (the golden Fleece, Belmont/Portia, has been won anyway). The image of Medea is one of her gathering enchanted herbs by the light of the moon. Are the two lovers in a state of enchantment? Should any of these images cast a shadow on how we play the relationship between Lorenzo and Jessica? However, there is one other element that we need to note in preparing to play this 'love' scene. On **line 14**, Lorenzo suddenly brings us into the world of here and now by reminding Jessica, and us the audience, of what Jessica did to bring her to this apparently happy state. Jessica responds by chiding Lorenzo for 'Stealing her soul with many vows of faith'. Lorenzo in turn declares that Jessica slanders him.

This is a small scene, but like so many small moments in this play, it needs to be approached with care and thought by the actors. The most obvious reading is to perform these exchanges as no more than a flirtatious foreplay between two lovers, and, by so doing, allow the actors playing Lorenzo and Jessica to establish themselves as a little more than marginal characters in the general narrative scheme. However, given the underlying tone of tragedy and betrayal in the classical references, and given the circumstances through which they contrived their marriage (and also with our knowledge of Jessica's father's demise, not yet revealed to them), we may wish to imbue the performance of this scene with a little more than a hint of *ennui* in order to suggest the possibility of an underlying emptiness in the relationship.

Whatever state of mood we have reached on stage by the end of this exchange, the mood is broken twice within the space of 23 lines (**25–48**): first, by the orderly arrival of Stephano, a messenger, with his news of Portia's imminent arrival; then by Launcelot Gobbo's disorderly arrival, stumbling around in the dark, and announcing the imminent arrival of his master Bassanio. Stephano's purpose is functional and serves to bring to a halt, momentarily, Lorenzo and Jessica's verbal foreplay, in order to announce that the real protagonists of this scene are about to make their appearance. Launcelot breaks into the reverie loudly and boisterously (**line 39**) and, by preventing Lorenzo and Jessica's exit (**line 36**), offers them another stage moment, albeit by default. We may be tempted, with some justification, to see this as the clown's (probably Will Kemp in the original production) last opportunity for a stage moment of improvisation and crowd-pleasing. And, by the fact that out of his seven lines, four of them are approximations of hunting calls, we may guess that Gobbo/Kemp was making the most of a tawdry piece of business that only required him to say that his master Bassanio was about to arrive. I have always been fascinated by the idea of improvisation on the Elizabethan stage where the 'text' is seen more as a 'script' or outline scenario, offering no more than an outline of what the clown may do on stage (think of Bottom and the Mechanicals in *A Midsummer Night's Dream* when they prepare their performance for the wedding of Theseus and Hippolyta). We may pause to wonder to what extent we may allow Launcelot Gobbo that opportunity, with, of course, a signal to the other performers as to when the written script is to recommence (rather as the solo performer signals the end of a cadenza in a concerto). However the Gobbo player may have handled the moment and to whatever extent the extant text records the moment on stage, he serves as an example of how to demonstrate (Bertolt Brecht would probably have used the verb 'narrate') to the audience, by his stumbling about, that he can't see where he is going because it is night time in the play (but, of course, daylight in the Elizabethan public theatre).

Lines 54–88 now afford Lorenzo and Jessica another opportunity to have the stage to themselves as Launcelot has, no doubt, bounced off the stage and Stephano will have made a dignified exit a few lines later. We have already remarked on the metatheatrical dimension to these lines. (Another way to describe this kind of moment in theatrical performance is to term it 'self-reflexive', which means that the performance draws attention to its theatricality by self-consciously 'framing' a moment in some way, as opposed to creating an illusion that sets out to convince the audience that this is really happening.) There is, however, one other element to Lorenzo's two speeches and Jessica's one-line response (**69**).

With music now playing on stage and Lorenzo's language sustaining a consistent iambic pentameter, the mood is still; the subject, the efficacy of music, by relating it to the harmony of the spheres: the musical harmony produced by the movement of the planets in the heavens. Jessica's line, 'I am never merry when I hear sweet music', could be because, as Lorenzo has just said, 'Such harmony is in immortal souls, / But whilst this muddy vesture of decay / Doth grossly close it in, we cannot hear it' (**lines 63–5**). If Jessica had spoken her line before Lorenzo gave his reason, we might understand how one image would lead to another. But, as she delivers it after the reason is given, Jessica's line assumes a rather distracted air. Is this a clue to the actor playing Jessica, to take her role for the rest of the scene in a direction different from the other's merriment? Does it offer the opportunity to the actor to be a silent commentator, remaining on stage after the others have entered the house?

The still contemplative mood is soon broken by the arrival of Portia and Nerissa. Portia comments on the light from the house, shining like 'a good deed in a naughty world' (**line 90**). We seem to be leaving the naughtiness (that is the wickedness) of Venice for the alternative world of Belmont. Whereas much of the play's action has taken place in a 'here and now' of mercantile ruthlessness, in all of its guises, the alternative world of Belmont awaits the narrative shift to romantic comedy.

But what is really going in these final lines of the play (**89–307**)? And what is required of the actors? The almost mystical primacy of the language of the Lorenzo and Jessica moments gives way to what amounts to a series of dirty jokes, and it is Portia who steps in with the first bawdy comment. What do the actors need to have in mind?

Portia and Nerissa are initially drawn into the atmosphere created by Lorenzo and Jessica, but on knowing that their husbands have not yet returned, Portia immediately assumes command and the pace of the scene quickens as Bassanio and dawn approach. The husbands must not know that they have been away – more to support the trick with the rings, than the fact that they were instrumental in saving Antonio's life (for that must be revealed anyway if the papers bearing various items of good news are to be revealed).

Bassanio enters in triumph, presumably having overheard Portia's last speech (**lines 124–6**, as his first lines (**127–8**) are clearly a response to Portia's. Where is Bassanio on stage in order to be able to hear Portia's remarks? On the original stage, as most of the business probably went on at what we would call 'down stage' amongst the audience, it is quite possible that Bassanio entered around **lines 120–1** through one of the 'up stage' doors and would be quite visible in a liminal space, neither off stage nor yet fully a part of the stage narrative. As he enters the stage business he is greeted by Portia in an uncharacteristically bawdy manner. Is this a new side to Portia of which the actor needs to take cognizance? In **lines 129–32** Portia manages to greet her husband, who believes he has not seen her for some time, with a joke that simultaneously carries on the image of (day)light as a pun, imbuing it with sexual innuendo regarding partners' positions in the act of sex. As Portia is greeting Antonio (who of course does not recognize her), Nerissa and Gratiano break into the moment, initiating the quarrel (at least it is a real quarrel for Gratiano, as it will be for Bassanio) over the rings. A sequence of events follows.

- Nerissa accuses Gratiano of having given the ring to a woman and the judge's clerk.
- Gratiano swears it was the judge's clerk, 'a little scrubbed boy, / No higher than thyself' (**lines 162–3**). Cue for knowing laugh from the audience.
- Portia intervenes (**lines 164–76**) to start sticking her knife in (she's good at this, if we cast our minds back to the trial) by declaring that she 'gave her love a ring' and that he swore never

to lose it. She is now controlling events once more and the actor needs to know this in order to decide at what level she wishes to play the humbling of her husband.

- Whereabouts on stage is Bassanio at this moment? We need to be able to see his reaction before he delivers his line to the audience: 'Why I were best to cut my left hand off, / And swear I lost the ring defending it' (**lines 177–8**).

- Gratiano, quick to implicate rather than defend his friend, leaps in to let Bassanio's 'cat out of the bag'. Should there be some level of gestural dispute going on between these two as this happens?

- *Pause* and *Silence* as Portia, still commanding the situation (Antonio, Lorenzo and Jessica have surely all but sunk into the background by now), turns to confront Bassanio with the lines, 'What ring gave you my lord? / Not that (I hope) which you received of me' (**184–5**). 'Not that (I hope)' is a moment any actor worth her comic timing should relish, particularly with the emphasis offered by the parentheses. How long should she hold the moment before giving the line? Portia could bark the line out and sharply twist her metaphorical knife. Or the actor, if she feels she could sustain the silence, could make the turn as slow as she likes, before giving the lines sweetly, but with the hint of menace we know she is capable of. The actor playing Bassanio will then have to work carefully with his response so as not to disrupt this opportunity for comic suspense.

- Bassanio's response is a lame one.

- Portia's reply (**189–91**) may be taken two ways. Either she is going to play the mock tragic figure (echoed by Nerissa), or she could deliver it with mock anger. Again a consistency of approach with what has happened and with what is to come over the rest of the scene.

- Bassanio is desperately attempting to recover the situation (**lines 192–8**). How should the actor deal with the language in this speech? Does the 'jingling' of lines, that is the beginning of lines and the ending of lines with the same word, give a clue as to what the actor may do?

- Portia, now riding high, drives the joke onwards, with her lines

being formed in a similar way to Bassanio's, but to a very different effect. She caps all with her final line (**208**), 'I'll die for't, but
some woman had the ring!' Surely a line half delivered to the
audience with a knowing wink. Another cue for knowing
laughter from the audience.

- Bassanio is cornered into telling the truth (**lines 209–22**).
- Portia responds by resorting to more bawdy humour and
  declaring that if all of this is true, she will sleep with the doctor
  (**lines 223–33**). She is enjoying herself (and her ability to
  control situations).
- The pressure increases as does Bassanio's misery with the to
  and fro of exchanges between the couple. There is only one
  interjection, and that a fairly feeble one, from Antonio (**line
  238**), otherwise the exchange between the two should be
  relentless on Portia's side with Bassanio buckling under the
  pressure.
- The final thrust of the joke. Portia gives Antonio a ring to give
  to Bassanio (by now she must have turned her back on him,
  feigning her disappointment in him as a husband) to replace
  the original. There is a final bawdy joke: Portia and Nerissa
  both claiming to have slept with the doctor and his clerk
  (which of course they have) – the last opportunity for Portia
  and Nerissa to enjoy their conspiracy with the audience; and
  final knowing laughter from the audience before the penny
  drops for Bassanio and Gratiano.
- Portia, the mistress of both Belmont and Venice, it would now
  seem, produces evidence that all of Antonio's argosies have
  come to port, and gives Lorenzo, via Nerissa, the news that he
  is to be the recipient of Shylock's wealth (some productions
  have so contrived this moment, **lines 288–93**, to make Jessica
  the recipient of the letter).
- The play ends with Gratiano's obscene punning couplet.

All is well according to the text, but is this how we see it today? I have
referred to the positions of Antonio and Jessica at the end of the play.
We may take the view that Antonio is well pleased with the restoration of his wealth (and more, if he is to receive some of Shylock's) and

that his melancholy is dissipated. How we represent Antonio at this moment will largely depend on how we created him from those very first melancholic lines, and, of course, how we perceive the relationship between him and Bassanio. Jessica, within the play's own terms, may be perfectly happy with her current position, but is that enough? We have noted all the problems through the play resulting from its attitudes towards Jews and Judaism, which while they may not have been a problem for the audience in the sixteenth century, do, undoubtedly, create difficulties for any of us considering a performance of *The Merchant of Venice* today. Short of changing the text of the play, which I, for one, would not advocate, we may consider adding to the play, not through the addition of text but through those gestural moments intrinsic to performance. The simple act of leaving Jessica alone on the stage may speak volumes in terms of framing the play's story.

The task of this chapter has not been to present an ideal notion of the play in production, but to open questions regarding the play's problems and its complexities. Sometimes knowing how to ask the significant question is of more use than finding the definitive answer.

Bibliography

Chapter 1: Textual History and Dates

Brown, John Russell (ed.), *The Merchant of Venice* (London: Arden Shakespeare, Methuen, 1967).

Eagleton, Terry, *Criticism and Ideology* (London: Basil Blackwell, 1978).

Edelman, Charles (ed.), *The Merchant of Venice* (Cambridge: Cambridge University Press, 2002).

Greg, W. W., *The Merchant of Venice, 1600 (Hayes Quarto)* (London: Shakespeare Association, 1939).

Greg, W. W., *The Shakespeare First Folio: Its Bibliographical and Textual History* (Oxford: Clarendon Press, 1955).

Holderness, Graham, *Textual Shakespeare: Writing and the Word* (Hatfield: University of Hertfordshire Press, 2003).

Rutter, Carol Chillington, *Documents of the Rose Playhouse* (Manchester and New York: Manchester University Press, 1999).

Stone, P. W. K., *The Textual History of 'King Lear'* (London: Scolar Press, 1980).

Thomson, Peter, *Shakespeare's Theatre*, 2nd edn (London: Routledge, 1992).

Thomson, Peter, *Shakespeare's Professional Career* (Cambridge: Cambridge University Press, 1992).

Thomson, Peter, 'Conventions of Playwriting', *Shakespeare: An Oxford Guide*, ed. Stanley Wells and Lena Cowen Orlin (Oxford: Oxford Univesity Press, 2003).

Wells, Stanley and Gary Taylor (eds), *The Oxford Shakespeare* (Oxford: Oxford University Press, 1986).

Williams, Gordon, *Shakespeare: Sex and the Print Revolution* (London: Athlone Press, 1996).

Williams, Raymond, *Marxism and Literature* (Oxford: Oxford University Press, 1997).

Chapter 2: Intellectual and Cultural Context

Blakemore Evans, G., *Elizabethan–Jacobean Drama* (London: A&C Black, 1987).

Brecht, Bertolt, *Brecht on Theatre: The Development of an Aesthetic*, trans. John Willett (London: Methuen, 1964).

Freedland, Arthur, *Preface to Philip Stubbes' The Anatomie of Abuses* (New York and London: Garland, 1973).

Greg, W. W. (ed.), *Henslowe's Diary, Parts I, II and III* (London: A. H. Bullen, 1904).

Gurr, Andrew, *The Shakespearean Stage, 1574–1642* (Cambridge: Cambridge University Press, 1980).

Hethmon, Robert H. (ed.), *Strasberg at the Actors' Studio* (New York: Viking Press, 1965).

Heywood, Thomas, *Early Treatises on the Stage* (London: Shakespeare Society, 1853).

Holderness, Graham, *Cultural Shakespeare: Essays in the Shakespeare Myth* (Hatfield: University of Hertfordshire Press, 2001).

Howard, Jean E., *The Stage and Social Struggle in Early Modern England* (London and New York: Routledge, 1994).

Irace, Kathleen O. (ed.), William Shakespeare, *The First Quarto of Hamlet* (Cambridge: Cambridge University Press, 1998).

Lotherington, John (ed.), *The Tudor Years* (London: Hodder & Stoughton, 1994).

MacPherson, David C., *Shakespeare, Jonson, and the Myth of Venice* (London and Toronto: Associated University Presses, 1990).

Morrill, John (ed.), *The Oxford Illustrated History of Tudor and Stuart Britain* (Oxford: Oxford University Press, 1996).

Nagler, A. N., *A Source Book in Theatrical History* (New York: Dover, 1952).

Nashe, Thomas, *Pierce Pennilesse, His Supplication to the Divell* – 1592 (London: Bodley Head, 1924).

Pendry, E. D. (ed.), *Thomas Dekker* (London: Edward Arnold, 1967).

Said, Edward W., *Culture and Imperialism* (London: Vintage, 1994).

Thomson, Peter, *On Actors and Acting* (Exeter: Exeter University Press, 2000).

Van Dorsten, J. A. (ed.), *Sir Philip Sidney: A Defence of Poetry* (Oxford: Oxford University Press, 1966).

Ward, Ian, *Shakespeare and the Legal Imagination* (London: Butterworth, 1999).

Weimann, Robert, *Shakespeare and the Popular Tradition in the Theater* (Baltimore and London: Johns Hopkins University Press, 1978).

Weimann, Robert, *Author's Pen and Actor's Voice: Playing and Writing in Shakespeare's Theatre* (Cambridge: Cambridge University Press, 2000).

Wickham, Glynne, Herbert Berry and William Ingram (eds), *English Professional Theatre, 1530–1660* (Cambridge: Cambridge University Press, 2000).

Chapter 3: Key Productions and Performances

Appleton, William W., *Charles Macklin: An Actor's Life* (Oxford: Oxford University Press, 1961).

Beauman, Sally, *The Royal Shakespeare Company: A History of Ten Decades* (Oxford: Oxford University Press, 1982).

Belford, Barbara, *Bram Stoker: A Biography of the Author of Dracula* (New York: Alfred A. Knopf, 1996).

Berry, Ralph (ed.), *The Methuen Book of Shakespeare Anecdotes* (London: Methuen, 1992).

Chambers, Colin, *Other Spaces: New Theatre and the RSC* (London: Eyre Methuen, 1980).

Collier, John Payne, *On the Death of the Famous Actor, Richard Burbage: Illustrations of Old English Literature*, vol. III (London: Private Printing, 1866).

Fitzgerald, Percy, *Henry Irving: A Record of Twenty Years at the Lyceum* (London: Chapman and Hall, 1893).

Fitzsimons, Raymund, *Edmund Kean: Fire from Heaven* (London: Hamish Hamilton, 1976).

Gross, John, *Shylock* (London: Chatto & Windus, 1992).

Holland, Peter, *English Shakespeares: Shakespeare on the English Stage in the 1990s* (Cambridge: Cambridge University Press, 1997).

Irving, Henry, *Impressions of America*, vol. I (London: Sampson and Rowe, 1884).

Lelyveld, Toby, *Shylock on the Stage* (Cleveland, Ohio: Western Reserve University Press, 1960).

Maclean, Catherine McDonald (ed.), *Characters of Shakespeare's Plays* (London: Dent, 1906).

Parry, Edward Abbott, *Charles Macklin* (London: Kegan Paul, 1891).

Playfair, Giles, *The Flash of Lightning* (London: William Kimber, 1983).

Sher, Antony, *Beside Myself* (London: Arrow Books, 2002).

Sinfield, Alan, 'Four Ways with a Reactionary Text', *Journal of Literature, Teaching, Politics, II* (University of Sussex, 1983).

Thomson, Peter, *On Actors and Acting* (Exeter: Exeter University Press, 2000).

Williams, Raymond, *Modern Tragedy* (London: Verso, 1979).

Chapter 4: The Play on Screen

Ansorge, Peter, 'Director in Interview', *Plays and Players*, 16 (March 1970).

Bulman, J. C. and H. R. Coursen (eds), *Shakespeare on Television* (Hanover and London: University Press of New England, 1988).

Davies, Anthony and Stanley Wells (eds), *Shakespeare and the Moving Image: The Plays on Film and Television* (Cambridge: Cambridge University Press, 1994).

Edleman, Charles (ed.), *The Merchant of Venice* (Cambridge: Cambridge University Press, 2002).

Hawkes, Terry, *Shakespeare's Talking Animals* (London: Edward Arnold, 1985).

Holderness, Graham, *Visual Shakespeare: Essays in Film and Television* (Hatfield: University of Hertfordshire Press, 2002).

Ryan, Kiernan, *Shakespeare* (Basingstoke: Palgrave Macmillan, 2002).

Chapter 5: Critical Assessments

Addenbroke, David, *The Royal Shakespeare Company* (London: Kimber, 1974).

Dollimore, Jonathan and Alan Sinfield (eds), *Political Shakespeare* (Manchester: Manchester University Press, 1985).

Drakakis, John (ed.), *Alternative Shakespeares* (London: Methuen, 1985).

Eagleton, Terry, *William Shakespeare* (Oxford: Blackwell, 1986).

Fortier, Mark, *Theory/Theatre: An Introduction* (London and New York: Routledge, 1997).

Freud, Sigmund, 'The Theme of the Three Caskets' (1913), *Shakespeare The Merchant of Venice: A Casebook*, ed. John Wilders (Basingstoke: Macmillan, 1969).

Greenblatt, Stephen, *Shakespearian Negotiations: The Circulation of Social Energy in Renaissance England* (Berkeley: University of California Press, 1988).

Hazlitt, William, *The Round Table and Characters of Shakespeare's Plays*, with Introduction by Catherine MacDonald Maclean (London: Dent, 1969).

Holderness, Graham, *Textual Shakespeare: Writing and the Word* (Hatfield: University of Hertfordshire Press, 2003).

Jameson, Fredric, *The Political Unconscious: Narrative as a Socially Symbolic Act* (Ithaca, NY: Cornell University Press, 1981).

Johnson, Samuel, *Preface 1765*, in *The Yale Edition of the Works of Samuel Johnson VII*, ed. Arthur Sherbo (New Haven and London: Yale University Press, 1968).

Laplanche, Jean and J. B. Pontalis, *The Language of Psychoanalysis* (New York: W. W. Norton, 1973).

Laqueur, Thomas, *Making Sex: Body and Gender from the Greeks to Freud* (Cambridge, MA: Harvard University Press, 1990).

Mendelson, Sara and Patricia Crawford, *Women in Early Modern England* (Oxford: Clarendon Press, 1998).

Ryan, Kieran, *Shakespeare* (Basingstoke: Palgrave Macmillan, 2002).

Said, Edward W., *Culture and Imperialism* (London: Vintage, 1994).

Sherbo, Arthur (ed.), *Johnson on Shakespeare* (New Haven and London: Yale University Press, 1968).

Smith, Bruce R., 'Studies in Sexuality', in *Shakespeare: An Oxford Guide*, ed. Stanley Wells and Lena Cowen Orlin (Oxford: Oxford University Press, 2003).

Ward, Ian, *Shakespeare and the Legal Imagination* (London: Butterworths, 1999).

Wells, Stanley and Lena Cowen Orlin, *Shakespeare: An Oxford Guide* (Oxford: Oxford University Press, 2003).

Wilders, John, *Shakespeare, The Merchant of Venice: A Casebook* (Basingstoke: Macmillan, 1969).

Williams, Raymond, *Problems in Materialism and Culture* (London: Verso, 1980).

Worthen, W. B., *Shakespeare and the Authority of Performance* (Cambridge: Cambridge University Press, 1997).

Chapter 6: Commentary

Barba, Eucenio, 'Theatre Anthropology in Action', *Théâtre International*, no. 1 (1981).

Banham, Martin, 'The *Merchant of Venice* and the implicit stage direction', *Critical Survey*, vol. 3, no. 3 (1991).

Barton, John, *RSC in Playing Shakespeare* (London: Methuen, 1984).

Brown, John Russell (ed.), *The Merchant of Venice* (London: Arden Shakespeare, Methuen, 1967).

Brown, John Russell, *Shakespeare and the Theatrical Event* (Basingstoke: Palgrave Macmillan, 2002).

Cookson, Linda and Brian Loughrey (eds), *Longman Critical Essays: The Merchant of Venice* (London: Longman, 1992).

Eagleton, Terry, *William Shakespeare* (Oxford: Basil Blackwell, 1986).

Ferris, Lesley (ed.), *Crossing: The Stage Controversies on Cross-dressing* (London and New York: Routledge, 1993).

Goodwin, John, *Royal Shakespeare Company, 1960–63* (London: Max Reinhardt, 1964).

Partridge, Eric, *Shakespeare's Bawdy* (London: Routledge & Kegan Paul, 1947).

Styan, J. L., *Shakespeare's Stagecraft* (Cambridge: Cambridge University Press, 1967).

Thomson, Peter, *On Actors and Acting* (Exeter: Exeter University Press, 2000).

Index